Living Your Colors

Living Your Colors

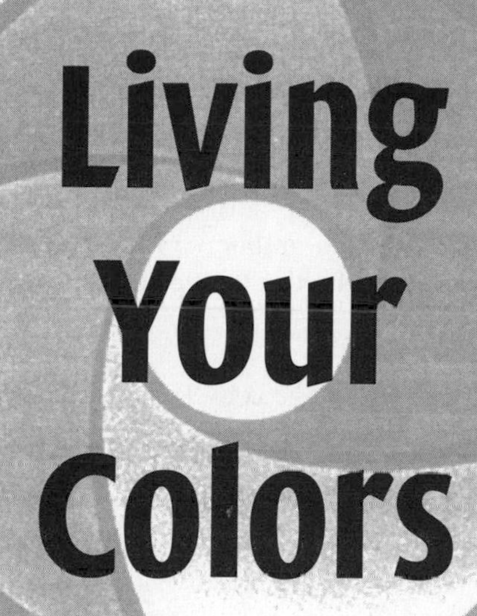

Practical Wisdom for Life, Love, Work, and Play

TOM MADDRON, M.S.

WARNER BOOKS

An AOL Time Warner Company

Warner Books, Inc., 1271 Avenue of the Americas, New York, NY 10020
Visit our Web site at www.twbookmark.com.

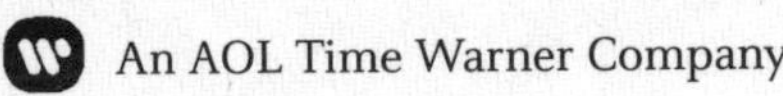

Library of Congress Cataloging-in-Publication Data
Maddron, Tom.
Living your colors : practical wisdom for life, love, work, and play / Tom Maddron.
p. cm.
ISBN 0-446-67911-9
1. Typology (Psychology) 2. Color—Psychological aspects. I. Title.

BF698.3 .M24 2002
155.2'64—dc21 2002025891

Book design by Fearn Cutler de Vicq

Printed in the United States of America

First Printing: December 2002

10 9 8 7 6 5 4 3 2 1

This book is dedicated to J. Krishnamurti whose writing, teaching, and conversation have opened so many hearts to the simple, loving observation of life and of human beings.

Acknowledgments

I would like to acknowledge the twenty-year partnership with Ed Forbes, LCSW, and Jeremy Howell, LCSW, which has resulted in the development of much material very helpful to human service professionals and to people in general. In addition, to my wife Margaret Maddron, M.Ed., I want to acknowledge our professional relationship that has greatly enriched all my efforts, and our marriage and friendship that have helped me to survive some very hard times with strength and joy. And to the thousands of Colors participants, thank you for making the Colors seminars a powerful opportunity for developing understanding of natural human differences.

Contents

CHAPTER 1

Assessing Your Colors

Welcome! This is a book about you . . . and about me. This is a book about personality styles. It is based on ancient traditional wisdom and also on modern research. The human patterns it reveals are natural, positive, and valuable. When you have assessed your own personality style and read about the styles of the important people in your life, you will have a new understanding and appreciation of the remarkable balance and harmony that is possible in human relationships. There are no wrong answers in your personal assessment. All the "Colors" are equally valuable and important. So enjoy! Celebrate the richness of human differences.

A "COLORS" QUIZ

Below you will find a questionnaire for determining your "Colors" profile. As you fill out the questionnaire, set aside what you've been told to be like and try to think of yourself as you are when you're most comfortable and natural.

Of course, we all have some of all these qualities, and they may come out more strongly at different times. For purposes of this quiz, however, try to look beyond specific situations, set aside what others think you "should" be like, look past the demands of your job, and forget for the moment about the requirements of your role in life. Just be yourself as you most naturally and comfortably are. *Please note:* Extra assessment sheets are provided at the back of the book.

Directions

In each of the 10 items,

- Put a **4** by the set of words that seems to describe you best.
- Put a **3** by the set of words that describes you second best.
- Put a **2** by the set of words that describes you third best.
- Put a **1** by the set of words that seems the least like you.

When you have completed the 10 items,

- Total the a's. Enter the a total beside "Gold" in the spaces provided at the bottom of the page.
- Total the b's. Enter the b total beside "Blue" in the spaces provided at the bottom of the page.
- Total the c's. Enter the c total beside "Green" in the spaces provided at the bottom of the page.
- Total the d's. Enter the d total beside "Orange" in the spaces provided at the bottom of the page.

Your highest totals indicate the Colors that you chose as being most like you in the quiz. Some people find that one or two Colors are really strong and the others very weak. Some people find that all four Colors are about equal in strength.

As you read on through the book, you may find changes in your sense of which Colors best describe you. You may feel that the relative weight of the Colors in your life is different than you thought or even than the quiz might suggest. Remember, you are always the best judge of what is right for you.

A Colors Quiz:

Rank the four sets of words in each item, **4, 3, 2, or 1** according to how well they describe you. **(4 is most like you.)**

1. a. ______ solid, steady, careful
b. ______ feeling, sympathetic, kind
c. ______ cool, clever, independent
d. ______ lively, witty, energetic

2. a. ______ reasonable, moral, hardworking
b. ______ sensitive, sincere, caring
c. ______ logical, abstract, moral
d. ______ skillful, playful, fun-loving

3. a. ______ dependable, faithful, devoted
b. ______ close, personal, involved
c. ______ curious, scientific, thoughtful
d. ______ daring, energetic, brave

4. a. ______ reliable, organized, serious
b. ______ peaceful, harmonious, warm
c. ______ impatient, perfectionist, heady
d. ______ here-and-now, impulsive, active

5. a. ______ consistent, structured, planned
b. ______ meaningful, spiritual, inspired
c. ______ analyzing, testing, model making
d. ______ high impact, persuasive, generous

6. a. _____ sane, faithful, supportive
b. _____ poetic, musical, artistic
c. _____ theoretical, studious, principled
d. _____ performing, playing, creating

7. a. _____ commit, follow through, persist
b. _____ communicate, encourage, nurture
c. _____ inform, discuss, question
d. _____ energize, compete, engage

8. a. _____ conserve, maintain, protect
b. _____ inspire, understand, appreciate
c. _____ design, invent, construct
d. _____ promote, excite, activate

9. a. _____ value, honor, provide
b. _____ share, connect, express
c. _____ respect, stimulate, dialogue
d. _____ touch, pleasure, surprise

10. a. _____ traditional, loyal, conservative
b. _____ belonging, involved, cooperative
c. _____ skeptical, nonconforming, fair
d. _____ free, independent, rebellious

Totals

a. Gold _____ **b. Blue** _____ **c. Green** _____ **d. Orange** _____

THE COLORS IN A NUTSHELL

	GOLD	BLUE	GREEN	ORANGE
Basic Need	Order	Authenticity	Rationality	Freedom
Strongest Values	Service Responsibility	Honesty Empathy	Objectivity Integrity	Action Individuality
Key Experience	Judgment	Emotion	Logic	Sensation
Learning Style	Concrete Organized Practical	Enthusiastic Cooperative Participatory	Independent Data-Based Analytical	Hands-On Skill-Based Physically Active
Greatest Joys	Accomplishment Service Recognition	Spiritual Insight Intimacy Love	Wisdom Discovery Innovation	Skill in Action Excitement Victory
Sexuality	Rewarding/Giving Private Fitting and Proper	Romantic Emotional Creative	Exploratory Inventive Thoughtful	Energetic Skillful Fun
Troubled By	Disorder Instability Lack of Responsibility	Disharmony Dishonesty Lack of Feeling	Illogic Injustice Sentimentality	Authority Regulations Pomposity
Encouraged By	Recognition of Contribution	Appreciation Emotional Support	Affirmation of Intelligence	Freedom Respect Applause
In Groups	Organization Commitment Follow-Through	Communication Inspiration Cooperation	Analysis Ingenuity Independence	Physical Skill Creative Energy Playfulness
On the Job	Stability Organization	Support Enthusiasm	Ingenuity Pragmatism	Energy Innovation
Personal Troubles	Overload Rigidity Bossiness	Moodiness Volatility Dreaminess	Indecisiveness Superiority Coldness	Carelessness Quick Temper Impulsiveness
Seeks in Relationships	Seriousness Responsibility Loyalty	Meaning Intimacy Affection	Autonomy Respect	Sensuality Excitement

CHAPTER 2

Introduction to Colors

THE POWER OF PICTURES AND STORIES

How we picture ourselves, how we tell the story of our lives, has a big effect on how we live. For example, if I ask you to list all your faults in one column and all your strengths in another, which will be easier? Which list will be longer? For some reason, most people's faults list is easier and longer. Maybe we fear being conceited. Maybe we are taught to be humble. The fact is, most of us are more aware of what's "wrong" with us than what is "right" with us. This book is about what is right with us.

There are many ways to be okay in this world. If there really were only one right way to be, very few of us would measure up to it, and we'd tend to be very judgmental about ourselves and others. We would argue and fight and exert pressure on one another to try to conform to that one right way. Fortunately, thank goodness, there are many right ways to be. The fundamental differences among us are natural. They complement one another and enrich our lives in many ways. When we tell our human story this way, so that human differences are natural and good, it relieves us of a lot of the need to be judgmental and frees us up to appreciate ourselves and each other in new ways.

This book is about this change in our pictures and stories about ourselves. It is about making small changes in our story now that will lead to big changes down the line. It is about an ancient idea, the idea of temperament. An idea taken from ancient Greece with surprising support from cultures the other side of the world, and from modern science.

This is not a book about "Truth." The four Colors, and the temperaments they represent, should be seen as a set of lenses for looking at the world. This is a very old set of lenses that has survived for thousands of years in more than one culture.

These lenses demonstrate certain natural differences among people. These natural differences can be appreciated and accepted. And as we all know only too well, these differences can also be argued about, rejected, and fought over.

The good news is that when we decide to appreciate and accept these natural differences, much of the trouble seems to go out of life. New understanding and new acceptance of others follow closely on the heels of a new attitude about the self—new pictures and stories. New pathways open up. Strengths are discovered. Limitations are accepted. Cooperation is improved. We move from conflict to an appreciation of our natural differences. This is the reason for this book. Little changes now. Big changes down the line.

THE HISTORY OF THE IDEA OF FOUR TEMPERAMENTS

The four Colors in this book are used to represent the four temperaments—which date back to the ancient Greeks in Europe. The early Greek philosophers of medicine identified four basic categories of human personality. They explained the categories in terms of a balance among the four bodily "fluids" that they believed were central to human health and behavior. When one of the personality types appeared, it was explained that a certain fluid was dominant.

As European science developed over the centuries, the idea of the four fluids was replaced by more sophisticated understanding of the body and of behavior. The idea of the four temperaments, however, survived. In the Yup'ik culture of western Alaska, one of the central religious symbols is called, in English, the Eye of Awareness. This symbol portrays the spirit acting through four basic elements that make us human. These elements are the body, the emotions, thinking, and culture or will.

The correlation between the old Greek ideas and the ancient Inuit culture is surprising and exciting. It suggests that temperament is something deeper than culture—something simply human.

In traveling and training across cultures, I have found this to be true. With the African American and Latino community of south-central Los Angeles, with the Yup'ik Eskimo community of western Alaska, with representatives of more than one hundred Native American tribes and villages from Alaska and the lower forty-eight states, with Asian Americans in the Central Valley of California, with exchange students from Southern African culture, and with European Americans of all ages and social classes, the Colors activity works just the same. A Yup'ik grandmother commented that doing Colors reminded her of listening in her childhood, many decades ago, to her own grandmother talking about "the different ways people choose to be."

The psychologist and philosopher, Carl Jung, made a major contribution to the idea of personality types when he published a book on the subject in 1921. Jung's work was taken up by Katherine Briggs and her daughter and son-in-law, Isabel Briggs and Peter Myers. This family effort resulted in the Myers-Briggs Personality Indicator, a popular and well-respected psychological test currently in use throughout the world.

In their book, *Please Understand Me,* psychologist David Keirsey and his co-author, Marilyn Bates, brought together the four temperaments of the Greeks with the sixteen personality types of the Myers-Briggs test. Whereas the Myers-Briggs Temperament Indicator is a highly defined, scientifically validated set of personality categories, *Colors* defines a flexible spectrum or profile, a rainbow of human qualities.

Over the centuries, these four elements of personality have interested people for the same reason that they interest us today. The four temperaments shed light on certain natural differences among people that make sense, differences that help us understand and relate to ourselves and the people around us.

Contemporary research, particularly some remarkable studies of identical twins, indicate that we are much less of a blank slate at birth than was once thought. The four temperaments are one way of describing some of our inborn personality differences—differences that don't seem to come from family or culture.

The Colors paint a picture of a human community made up of natural and complementary strengths, strengths that can work together to do wonderful things. The Colors also shed light on the endless conflicts, difficulties, and misunderstandings that are common to all cultures throughout history.

This book gives you comprehensive, accessible, and useful information about the temperaments. It is written in language much of which came directly from people just like you. I have carried out Colors seminars with more than eight thousand people, and their words echo through the practical wisdom of *Living Your Colors.*

The Colors provide a flexible profile, a rainbow of human qualities. Whether in romance, family, work, or friendship, the insights in this book are easy to understand and to remember. You will recognize yourself and the people around you on every page. In addition, *Living Your Colors* focuses on what is good, strong, and valuable about our personalities. This is no catalog of sins, but rather a celebration of the miracle of balance that gives the human community such flexibility and adaptability, that has contributed so much to our successes and our future possibilities.

THE FOUR COLORS

It is important to remember that the pure Colors do not exist. They are more like compass points in a map of human personality traits. Studying the four Colors builds a remarkable familiarity with the natural differences among people. Some of us are very close to one of the compass points. Some of us are near the center of the compass, with elements of all the directions.

Put simply, the influence of the four elements can be described as follows: Some of us lead with our hearts; some with our physical bodies and sensations; some, with our analytical thinking minds; and some, with our judgments and standards.

- **Gold.** Those of us who lead with judgment and standards show the characteristics of what we call the Gold personality style.

- **Blue.** Those of us who lead with our hearts show the characteristics of what we call the Blue personality style.
- **Orange.** Those of us who lead with our physical skills and sensations show the characteristics of what we call the Orange personality style.
- **Green.** Those of us who lead with our analytical thinking minds show the characteristics of what we call the Green personality style.

WHAT IF I SEEM TO HAVE SOME OF ALL THESE COLORS?

Naturally, each of us is a blend of all these characteristics. In fact, the word *temperament* comes from a Greek word meaning "mixture." Each of us is really a rainbow of Colors.

Sometimes we may be more Blue; our hearts may be more active and alive, and everything may seem personal and full of feeling.

Sometimes we may be more Orange—more physical, energetic, and impulsive.

Sometimes we may be more Green—more reserved, deliberate, and analytical.

Sometimes we may be more Gold—more organized, traditional, committed, and practical.

Still, it's important to notice that most of us have a strong, underlying style, a certain combination of the Colors, that stays with us . . . perhaps even throughout our lives.

This underlying style is really positive, fundamental, and long-lasting. We can let go of the constant effort to change it. We can accept our temperament and learn to live with it successfully, rationally, fully, and beautifully.

Just as important, we can let go of the effort to change the personalities of the other people in our world. We can learn to live with them as they are.

WHAT ABOUT RELATIONSHIPS?

Chapter 8 focuses on the six basic relationships among the four Colors. The Colors are a great help in understanding the complicated field of relationships in which we find ourselves. It's interesting to think about how these relationships work.

I start with a relationship with myself . . . I and myself . . . how I wish to be and how I am.

Then there is my relationship toward others . . . I and you, I and they . . . how I wish to be seen and accepted.

In addition, others have ways of relating to me . . . they see me a certain way, they act toward me a certain way . . . a world of people around me.

Lastly, I care about how others are relating to each other around me . . . fussing and feuding, loving and harmonious . . . I affect their relationships, and their relationships affect me.

It goes in circles. Let's say that my Blue side meets my Gold side. They work together, they argue and discuss, I make a decision. I talk to you about it, and my Blue/Gold decision runs smack into your Green/Orange point of view. You react to me in a certain way. Perhaps we disagree. So you go talk to John and Mary about it. John agrees with you. Mary agrees with me. You and John agree with each other, and you both argue with Mary. Mary sends me flowers, and John sends me a brick. I begin to doubt myself or to feel good about myself. Maybe I change my decision. Maybe I stick to it. And so the wheel turns.

WHY DO THE COLORS SEEM SO REAL AND ACCURATE?

When they first look at their Colors, people are often shocked to find very personal and private thoughts, feelings, and experiences described so accurately. After many years of working with Colors, however—after seeing so many people go through the seminar activity—I no longer find it a mystery why Colors works so well. It is a simple way of sorting out the world of human experience. It's based on the idea that there are four very basic elements that shape human experience and behavior, four basic psychological functions.

Once these elements are selected and identified, it becomes apparent that each person presents a different mixture, a different balance of the functions. Some people are very much influenced by one or two of the Colors. Others show a balance among three or four. These preferences lead to natural and understandable differences in how people see the world and how they behave in it.

HOW CAN I LEARN TO RECOGNIZE AND UNDERSTAND THE COLORS?

For most of us, the best method of learning is to read, observe, and talk over these differences with other people in our daily life. A good Colors training or seminar can give us the opportunity to see the Colors in action. But there's nothing like daily life as a laboratory to watch the Colors unfold.

There's nothing like seeing ourselves mirrored in our relationships with others who have a similar temperament. There's nothing like seeing the range of familiar differences that show up in family, friends, acquaintances, coworkers, fictional characters, movie actors, politicians, and all the great parade of human types that we see throughout our lives.

THE PAYOFF!

My years of study of these natural differences have brought about a great change in me. A very positive change. I wish the same for you. The best part is that I no longer feel that people are setting out to annoy me with their contrary ways. I no longer feel the need to get into disputes with others about ways of being. I now see myself and the personalities around me as the natural working out of these four basic human elements, and it all makes sense!

All in all, I now see the world as a magical blend of personal styles, strengths, and relationships. I love the Yup'ik idea that we are all spirit at the center and that our differences arise from the four natural elements. As I watch it all work out, I see that we can accomplish just about anything if we learn to accept our natural, inevitable, and valuable differences and get on with *Living Our Colors.*

COLORS REVEALED

Keep in mind that each of us can be seen as a blend of the four Colors, a rainbow or spectrum, a "mixture" in that ancient meaning of the word *temperament.* The pure Colors don't exist. Some of us, however, are very strongly one way or another. Very Gold. Very Blue. Very Orange. Very Green. Some of us are a balanced mixture of three or four of the Colors. Most of us fall somewhere in between.

In understanding people, it is always helpful to know their first two Colors, at least. A Gold/Orange person may act quite differently from a Gold/Green or a Gold/Blue person. The three will have similarities due to having the Gold in common, though, each of the three will be very different according to his or her Color.

In learning to think about Colors, it is helpful to separate out and heighten the differences among the four. In the next four chapters, we will look at the very Gold Golds, the very Blue Blues, the very Orange Oranges, and the very Green Greens. Later on we will look at the six basic pairs of Colors, both as they interact with each other, and as they work out together, blended in one person.

Read on! I know you'll be glad you did.

CHAPTER 3

GOLD

Protect and Serve

"Tradition, good order, and good work"

I am solid, traditional, hardworking, and productive. I use my skills and energy to help things work out and go well. I like things to run smoothly.

I respect the wisdom that has been handed down in customs and traditions. I need security in my work and in my relationships.

I know that love means loyalty and responsibility. It's very easy for things to get muddled up and to fall apart, so I take good care to keep it all together.

I make plans and lists and I follow through on them. I am on time and cooperative in groups. I try to get other people to get with the program, but I often end up carrying most of the load. People depend on me.

I try to measure up to high standards, and I feel guilty when I don't meet them. I'm pretty successful, and I do it the old-fashioned way: "I earn it!"

Gold. What the Greeks called the melancholic temperament. What the Yup'ik Eskimos describe as spirit acting through culture and duty.

Golds judge the world according to standards of excellence. These standards are carried over from past experiences. The past may be ten centuries ago or ten minutes ago, but it is the solid Gold's best and surest source of wisdom and best guide for action.

Standards may evolve and change to some degree, but for Golds the underlying values are eternal . . . hard work, duty, responsibility, commitment, order. These are the things that give life meaning and make it livable.

Golds' standards and principles form a mental and emotional map. The map gives order to life and shapes how things are seen. When new things are discovered, they are examined in comparison to the best of the past, and corrections are made in an effort to help things measure up to the standard.

This correction of things toward the standard is one of Golds' most important contributions. Extreme Golds see criticism as a sacred duty, an obligation to serve quality. Rarely does anything seem perfect just as it is. Improvement is always possible, therefore it is always possible to make a contribution toward improvement.

For Golds, this process of correction and improvement is a positive thing, one of the most positive. Of course, the other Colors often complain and accuse Golds of being negative and overly critical. But for Golds, praise seems to be deserved only rarely. Worse yet, easy praise is actually a threat to quality and therefore to order and stability. It would be insincere and possibly even destructive to give praise just to make others feel better. Easy praise tarnishes the standard, and the standard is most important.

We have all heard that judgment is a two-edged sword, and it certainly cuts both ways for Golds. Having high standards for others is just part of having high standards for themselves. These high standards expose the Golds to much stress and guilt. Their own failures to measure up are much more painful to them than the failures of others, and a nagging sense of never being quite "up to snuff" is a common Gold complaint.

Golds experience life as basically unstable. It needs constant effort and attention to keep from deteriorating into chaos and confusion. The ground underfoot never seems to be quite solid. The shelter overhead is always threatening to leak. The picnic will bring ants. The parade will bring rain.

So Golds bring the bug spray and umbrellas. They prepare, provide, and give care. They never want to be on the receiving end. To be needy and dependent is a horror to Golds. Lists, priorities, plans, agreements, contracts, institutions, rituals, roles, and authority are ways Golds use to keep order, to stem the tide of chaos that always threatens to overwhelm. Left on its own, life goes downhill.

These basic concerns combined with high standards of order and quality lead to a pretty serious approach to life. Golds are noted for their seriousness, for their sense of duty and obligation, and for their sense of place.

Golds believe in institutions. They are not satisfied with patchwork and improvisation. The fundamentals must be sound. Punctuality is crucial. Concrete outcomes and accomplishments count. Dreams and plans have no substance until they are executed and the paperwork is complete. "The day's work counts!"

The social order is very fragile, and a proper network of obligations, duties, and roles provides the only possible security. Love and affection are too fleeting and untrustworthy to be relied upon. Energy and enthusiasm are passing things. Intellectual analysis often undermines order. It is loyalty, duty, authority, and reward and punishment that keep things from falling apart. Public opinion, status, and proper appearances are not incidental. They are essential.

This means work before play, and the play is likely to be well organized and productive, too. Exercise for health. Travel to broaden the mind. Not just skiing, but being on the ski patrol. Responsible play, a Red Cross backpack, and free ski-lift tickets, too! Sex in its proper place, well deserved, giving and receiving, a heaven-sent relief from the toils and tribulations of maintaining order and productivity, a sign of commitment and the natural order of love.

Of all the Colors, Golds have the hardest time ever going on vacation. If there's a phone nearby, they report that they might as well be at the office. If they can be reached, or even if they could call in, they are really not "away." And when they do manage to get really "away"—say, on a white-water rafting trip—thoughts of the mess that is building up at the office are never far from their minds. Golds know that the price of vacation will be the cleanup afterward.

This isn't just how Golds see the world. It's usually how it actually works. The other Colors count on Gold to carry the load, and the Golds oblige in order to get things done and to get them done "right." It's a circular process, and the other Colors are quite content as the burdens shift toward the Golds. Everyone knows that the Golds will carry the burdens if humanly possible. Everyone counts on that.

This means Golds are always at risk of being overloaded and even overwhelmed. Worst of all, they try not to show it. They try to tough it out like the Stoics of old. Always careful about appearances, Golds often tighten up their image as the pressure mounts. They may look their best just before they go over the edge. The cues may be subtle and indirect—weight loss or gain; paleness; dark circles under the eyes; illness.

In a troubled family or organization, the Gold will be trying to keep it all together. The child trying to parent the parents. The grandmother trying to keep a disintegrating family from self-destructing. The business partner in the shaky business, burning the midnight oil, struggling to keep the ship afloat.

We must protect and care for our Golds. They look strong, and they are reluctant to ask for help. We'd better help them anyway, without being asked, if we want them to survive to continue to make their contribution.

One way to help is to pay attention. Golds are supported and enlivened by public recognition. It needs to come spontaneously, and it must be earned. A word of recognition, a pat on the back . . . or much better yet, a plaque, a bonus, and a raise. Real, concrete recognition and a job well done—these are among the highest joys for Golds.

The flip side of this need for recognition is a common Gold experience of bitterness based on slights, lack of respect, and lack of recognition. The difficulty that the other Colors experience with Golds' authoritarian style often leads to criticism and resistance or simply to silence rather than respect and acknowledgment.

Money has a special place for Golds. They often report that earning money is better than finding money or winning money, that they have rarely if ever overdrawn a checking account, that they prefer to accumulate money rather than spend it, that money means more to them than merely the power to buy—it's a concrete symbol that they are doing all right as people, and that there is some degree of security for the future.

Across cultures, the Golds are the caretakers of the traditions, the ceremonies, the ways of the community. They show deep respect for their elders and for the proper authorities of the established order. They resist and reject revolutionary ideas and often are deeply suspicious of things that are new or the influences of other cultures.

Strong Golds can be quite fierce and even warlike in defense of their community. This can be true whether the community is an ancient religious heritage, a country, an ethnic group, or a family tradition.

Gold Dislikes

Golds see much in the world that does not measure up to their generally high ideals and their belief in traditional standards. Perfection is very rare. Flaws and imperfections stand out. Golds tend to see things as they should be, and the reality rarely measures up.

Golds understand that order is fragile and that chaos awaits around every turn. Their high need for security and stability leads to a deep concern about anything that threatens orderly living. When the ground is shaky underfoot, the Gold experiences very real anxiety. The anxiety leads to dislike of anything eccentric or revolutionary.

Golds are committed to hard work, productivity, success, and the smooth running of institutions and procedures. Punctuality and adherence to routine are high values. Anything that seems to threaten these values is met with intense dislike. Nonconformity, insubordination, disobedience, and irresponsibility head the list of threats to order. Confronted with these things, the Gold will complain and criticize.

Confusion is a Gold nemesis. One of the main contributors to confusion is a lack of clear leadership with clearly defined roles for the leader and the follower. Golds see definite hierarchy and legitimate authority as essential in avoiding confusion and getting the job done. They abhor a power vacuum, confused and uncertain leadership, or no leadership at all. Unclear expectations and fuzzy goals are simply impossible to deal with.

Golds tend to have many strong dislikes. They are often rather grumpy. They experience a lot of guilt and the burdens of responsibility, and may be annoyed by cheerfulness and playfulness in others. Slobs, procrastinators, and idlers are of no use to Golds.

CHAPTER 4

BLUE

Create Harmony

"True feelings and real relationships"

I lead with my heart and dream of a better world. I feel things deeply, both joy and pain. I love to discover beauty in people and in nature. I love to nurture and care for people and things and watch them grow. I'm very romantic.

Personal relationships are important to me. Honest sharing and real communication are some of the highest things in life. Being with other people can be hard, especially when they are selfish and uncaring.

I always try to make peace, but I would rather be alone than be with people who can't or won't get along. I am sometimes moody, and old feelings and experiences from the past stay with me a long time.

I always want to find the best in people. I value cooperation and goodwill. I am interested in spiritual things. I wish for "the peace that passeth understanding."

Blue. What the Greeks called the choleric temperament. What the Yup'ik describe as spirit seeing and acting through emotion.

Blues swim in a sea of feelings. They are usually quite good at this kind of swimming, accepting and flowing with emotions that would thoroughly upset the other Colors. Of all the Colors, however, extreme Blues most often report that they wish they were some other Color. They often wistfully admire the Oranges with their carefree grace and playfulness, the Golds for their orderliness, and the Greens for their cool heads. But Blues find themselves destined to live with the joys and sorrows of being the deeply feeling Color.

The heart is a sensitive and powerful instrument for Blues. It registers all the subtleties and nuances of relationships as well as all the ups and downs of the personal self. Joy and pain, pangs and twinges of eagerness or shyness, a constant music of emotional sensation accompany every aspect of daily life.

These emotions are as real as a toothache for Blues, deep physical sensations that cannot be ignored. The other Colors often misunderstand, believing that the Blues are "thinking" these emotions, "acting as if" these personal and relational things were important, "deciding" to be this way. Not so.

For Blue, a heartache is a bodily sensation, as real as a broken arm. Inspiration and enthusiasm flood the body with emotional energy. Fear is a consuming physical presence. Shame reddens the face and brings tears, and tears are never far away for Blues. Love and sympathy are all-consuming.

Parting is no sweet sorrow for Blues. Every good-bye is a loss, often filled with anxiety and sadness. The other Colors are sometimes confused by Blue's careful attention to the little partings and separations that are so frequent in daily life. A very Blue family might gather at the window to wave good-bye when some family member leaves for the grocery store! My own family, for example.

Rage is fierce for Blues, fiercer perhaps than for any other

Color. Often this rage comes from another particularly Blue characteristic, the hatred of injustice. Everything is personal to Blues, and persons are precious. All fragile things are precious. When a Blue sees a child being badly treated, an animal abused, nature trampled, social injustice, sorrow easily gives way to righteous anger. Though the fuse is long, it is a big bang.

Self-righteousness is a Blue specialty. Since they are particularly sensitive to the subtleties of personality, Blues know where other people are vulnerable. When the self-righteous rage does come out, Blues often go for the jugular of the person they are attacking. Blues are so averse to conflict that when they do go to war, they usually try to go for a single knockout punch in the first round. "The she-bear and her cubs." Beware the angry Blue.

The Blue's sensitivity makes a wonderful contribution to the community. Blues are enthusiastic, generous, and inspiring. They are process-oriented, and they want to bring out the best in others. Warm and sympathetic, they are good at promoting smoothly flowing relationships and at bringing out the full participation of all group members. They love to nurture things, groups, people, and watch them grow.

In intimate relationships, Blues are very romantic and attach great meaning to small gestures, gifts, sweet nothings, and tokens of affection. Sex expresses loving and caring. It is part of Blues' endless search for self-expression and self-realization and may be very creative. It usually reflects the kind of intimacy that takes place between two people. Blues may feel deeply betrayed if their sexual partner finds such intimacy with another person. They are prone to getting into relationships they can't seem to get out of—even when they want to—for fear of hurting the other person.

Blues feel conflict coming a mile away and try to finesse it before it happens. Usually very flexible, Blues will set aside their own interests and ideas in service to group harmony. They easily adopt a nonjudgmental attitude and are keenly aware of the points of view of others. All this flexibility and goodwill can come to a screeching halt, of course, when the Blue is out of sorts, self-righteous, and resentful.

Blues tend to be intuitive and good with words. Natural and effective communicators, they are skillful at getting their point across in a variety of ways. Their idealism combines with their natural enthusiasm, and they strive to influence others to a better life, often a spiritual life, a self-actualized life.

Blues account for a small percent of the total population. They are, however, naturally drawn to helping professions and other influential occupations. In education and social-service settings, Blues are often in the majority, along with the Golds.

Blues often believe that the Blue way of life is the healthy way of life. They see intimacy and emotion as the keys to health and happiness, and they urge these values on the people around them. Greens, Golds, and Oranges are sometimes made to feel that their ways are wrong, even that there's something wrong with them as people.

Blues' sensitivity can work against them. They sometimes see themselves as pathologically undefended: no armor, no facade, no mask. It is remarkable how often Blues speak of feeling "crushed." This is a special word for Blues. It means feeling inwardly devastated by personal failures, slights, misunderstandings, or mistreatment, real or imagined.

Encouragement and emotional support are crucial for Blues. Left on their own without any feedback from others, they usually assume the worst. Other people's silence is interpreted as negative, and Blues spiral down in their feelings.

Criticism is also hard for Blues to take. Since everything is personal, criticism is personal. Blues don't naturally separate themselves from their actions, so criticism of actions is criticism of self. None of the other Colors is so vulnerable about this issue. To Oranges, put-downs and competition are natural, even fun. To Golds, criticism of self and others is a sacred responsibility, the key to maintaining high standards. To Greens, skepticism and critical judgment mean intellectual rigor, and they thrive on the precision that results. For Blue, criticism just means failure.

This fragility of the self is a key to the Blue temperament. Not only are persons precious, they are fragile and unique. Hurt feelings are real hurts. The consequences last a long time. This fragility breeds anxiety. Blues do not heal quickly from emotional hurts. For Blues, all emotional experience lasts a long time, with feeling memories often carried from early childhood into the last stages of life with the full emotional load intact.

Loss, emotional trauma, and betrayal are not going to be gotten over easily for Blues. When the other Colors are ready to move on into the future or just into the here and now, the Blue is still in the throes of the past. To some degree, this must simply be accepted. Skillful grief work, artistic expression, careful communication, and good therapy may all have their place, but the fact is that, for Blue, feelings from the past will always be easily resuscitated and brought to life.

Fragility goes hand in hand with the constant Blue quest for meaning, for actualization and the highest possible realization of self. The quest for spiritual awareness, for transcendent understanding, for direct awareness of highest things is a common denominator for Blues.

To some extent, this quest is fostered by the intensity of suffering that Blues endure in the rough-and-tumble of daily life. The heart that feels great pain is capable of great joy. The suffering of Jesus, the Sufi's wine of love, the compassion and joy of the Chassidic Jewish tradition, the peace that passeth understanding, all the ecstatic religious paths have great appeal. For the Blue, the goals of religion are freedom, realization, and direct experience, rather than dogma, ethics, or morality.

Blues are often on a mission, driven by a utopian ideal or a meaningful experience. Though sometimes overly romantic and unrealistic, Blues often bring real vision to the community. With a global perspective, looking beyond facts and actions, Blues often bring a view of the whole and of great possibilities.

Blue Dislikes

Blues' dislikes grow out of their special concern for relationships, the intensity of their feelings, and their deep commitment to the sanctity of persons.

Unpleasant emotional experiences are a frequent occurrence for Blues, and they will go to great length to avoid them. Blues have long feeling memories. Emotional events are remembered, and the power of the feelings comes back along with the details of who, what, when, where, and why. Bad sex is as bad as it gets, leaving its traces for years to come. Their strong reactions include a kind of hysteria, as well as that remarkable Blue rage.

Very high on the list of dislikes for most Blues is hypocrisy or insincerity. Blues are outraged by people who put on the appearance of virtue, generosity, or kindliness while contradicting these appearances in their behavior.

Injustice and exploitation are deeply troubling to Blues. Being in the presence of unfairness or hurtful behavior is just about more than a Blue can stand.

A list of Blue dislikes would include: deception, insincerity, artificiality, competition, domination, impersonalness, disharmony, lack of feeling, dishonesty, emotional coldness, injustice, stress and conflict, judgmental people, rigid structure, lack of communication, isolation, detail work, being yelled at, cruelty of any kind, bossy negative people, heartlessness, and compulsiveness.

CHAPTER 5

ORANGE

Just Do It!

"Moving. Happening. Going. Doing."

I want to be free to act. I want to make things happen. I love to be good at lots of things. I love to compete with others and do my best. I love to win!

I don't understand how people can sit around all day and endlessly talk, talk, talk. Life is an adventure. Action and excitement are the spice of life. I want to move, and laugh, and achieve things. I want to be with people who want to do things.

I'm impulsive and spur-of-the-moment. Too much planning, too much seriousness, too much thinking—they all get in the way of living now! I want to be respected for my skill, my creativity, and my energy.

Live and learn, that's what I say. Learn by doing. Hands on. Then do something with it, for heaven's sake, or what's the point?

Now, what did you say was the next activity? Let's get going!

Orange. What the Greeks called the sanguine temperament. What the Yup'ik describe as spirit seeing and acting through the body.

When it's time to ride the rocket, Orange will be the first to volunteer. Others may provide the vision, the design, the detail work and organization, but Orange will fly the machine with skill and daring.

Action and sensation are the keys to the Orange experience, the life of the senses and the physical body. Orange seems to make up about a third of the population, equal in percentage to Gold, making Orange and Gold the two predominant Colors. This means that physical action is an influence equal to order and tradition in the human community.

From shaking the slats of the crib to rocking a chair over backward in a grade school classroom, riding a motorcycle on two-lane blacktop, starting an independent business, and building a house from the ground up without any blueprint, Orange must act!

This action is not a decision. It doesn't stem from an idea, a philosophy, or an emotion. It comes from the actual muscular and hormonal energy of the body. Thinking about it, explaining it, giving reasons for it—these come later. In the beginning is action.

This intense, physical demand for action leads to an absolute need for freedom. If forced to sit still and listen for long, the knee begins to bounce up and down, the pencil waggles in the fingers, the hands beat out a rhythm under the table, the mind wanders, sleepiness sets in, and various ideas begin to pop up about ways to generate some entertainment.

Some Oranges are quiet in their demeanor, physically still. But the inner experience is the same. Energy, impatience, restlessness, action for its own sake, the desire to *do* something!

Life without enjoyment simply makes no sense to Orange.

What is all this seriousness, routine, and drudgery for, anyway? Is there something wrong with delight, excitement, and play? Or sex? What about the development of skill entirely for its own sake, getting really good at something just because you can, acting for the sheer joy of it? And why should everything have a reason, a purpose, a meaning? Can't things just exist for their own sake? Okay, so we need to get in enough food for the winter. Let's at least whistle while we work!

Needless to say, Orange meets with some difficulty in dealing with the orderly Gold and Blue worlds of school and of various occupations, with their demands for conformity and physical restraint. Commitments and obligations often have the same stultifying effect.

Thus *freedom* becomes a key word for Orange. The experience of being bound, of being held still or tied down is too unpleasant. It is a real and powerful suffering, an explosive physical discomfort, and it must be avoided as much as possible.

When this demand for freedom turns into a battle with the other Colors, as it sometimes does, Orange can become really rebellious, oppositional, and defiant. Green's reasons, Blue's emotions, and Gold's duties are like words in a foreign language to an Orange who needs to move, and move now.

Extreme Oranges live in the here and now. Urges, whims, and impulses don't happen in a long field of past, present, and future. They occur now, and now is what there is. This gives these impulses great power and reduces the power of restraints.

Self-control, organization, limits, boundaries, plans—none of these things comes naturally for Oranges. They need external structure. They need someone to tap them on the shoulder and mention that, at their current speed, they won't make it around the next curve. This is Oranges' deepest dilemma. They may need help in dealing with the high level of organization required by modern school, work, and life in general. Yet while such help with external structure is needed, it may be very hard to accept.

But what a contribution Oranges make to the community . . . ! Energy, skill, charisma, grace, accomplishment, laughter, competition, spirit, play, camaraderie, creativity . . . all these and more enliven the group, generate action, and prevent stagnation.

Oranges thrive on crisis, handling it with skill, sometimes even generating it when they feel that things need to be shaken up. They are tool handlers, often mechanically inclined, with a high tolerance for discomfort and intense effort.

Oranges like to work and play in teams with a strong sense of team loyalty and camaraderie. They make work into play. They handle projects well when they are given specific goals, timelines, and outcomes but are left to get the work done on their own. They are strong negotiators. They are self-starters and long-distance runners—when the incentives are right and they are truly engaged.

Oranges develop alternative lifestyles, lifestyles that give free rein to the spontaneity, creativity, energy, and impulsiveness that is their natural style. In the arts, skilled crafts, performance, sports, sales and marketing, or entrepreneurship of all kinds, Oranges often create unique roles for themselves within or outside the system.

They are rarely interested in broad, liberal-arts intellectual pursuits, or in knowledge for its own sake. When they get to college, they often outperform everyone. They chose it, they know why they're there and what they want out of it. They are self-motivated and bring all their energy to bear on the outcome they want. Oranges want to learn by doing and achieve concrete results. Once again, immediacy takes the place of long-term goals and objectives, and the Orange heads out into the job market or into an alternative lifestyle that lets him or her be free.

It's important to note that there are many Orange women. Just as the Blue man may have difficulties due to macho cultural stereotypes, the Orange woman may struggle with female stereotypes of all kinds. Blue and Gold women often find that their temperaments lead them in directions more traditionally "female." Orange and Green women, with their tendencies toward physical adventure and intellectual coolness, often see themselves as marching to a different drummer when it comes to matters of gender.

But Oranges usually love to challenge limits anyway. Orange women are physically skillful, energetic, spontaneous, competitive, often humorous or even sarcastic, and it is a delight to see the many interesting roles and lifestyles that they develop for themselves.

For both male and female Oranges, sex is just about the most exciting and fun activity in life. They approach it with great good humor and with the characteristic freedom and creativity that marks everything they do. They do not see sex as tangled up with all kinds of sober relationship issues, but as a joy in its own right.

On the other side of the coin, Oranges often conceal their nature from others who do not understand, or who judge them negatively. One of the joys of a Colors activity is to watch people from each Color discover their strength and worth—*and* those of all the other Colors. The Oranges often show this the most of all as they come into their own with pride and self-respect.

Orange Dislikes

For Oranges, the world needs to be a free-play zone. All their strengths—spontaneity, energy, creativity, enthusiasm—depend on having room to move. When they are confined and constrained, their dislikes are intense. And given their action-oriented nature, Oranges are inclined to rebel against what frustrates them.

Overstrict and rigid authority usually leads the list of things most hated by Oranges. The strong hand holding them back simply makes no sense to them. To Oranges, control often seems to be arbitrary and unreasonable. It feels to them as if someone were simply trying to dominate them, to defeat them in a power struggle. Oranges do not like to be told what to do or not to do. They don't like pompous people, and they will not be condescended to.

When Oranges are seriously out of sorts they may become rude and aggressive, dismissive, and harsh in their communication.

Routines and boredom fall right in alongside rigid authority as a burr under the Orange's saddle. It is a physical agony for Orange to have to do the same rote task over and over again. Boredom is not just a state of mind for Orange. It is a physical discomfort of major proportions. The muscles fill up with thwarted energy, which finds its way into all kinds of restless activity and ultimately to an explosive release. Oranges become very good at finding ways to release this energy, turning work into play, making a competitive game of a task, or stirring up playfulness in their relationships.

While Oranges will practice endlessly a skill or behavior that interests them—a jump shot, a musical scale, the effective use of a tool, a game strategy, a sales gambit, a dance step—it is their interest, their creativity, and their active participation that drive them. The imposed routine of no immediate interest or reward drives them crazy.

Just as difficult as rote and routine is the challenge of having to be physically still. The classroom can be a trial. The lecture hall, a torture chamber. The desk, a prison. The library, a tomb.

Equally tough is the lack of a real challenge. The Orange thrives on challenge, on novelty, and on reaching for new heights of performance. An easy task is of no interest unless it pays well. A long string of easy tasks leads to boredom and the search for something new.

In general, Oranges don't like interruptions, rigid timelines, paperwork and bureaucracy, rigid people, slow people, slow drivers (!), standing in lines, too much talk, couch potatoes, negativity, lack of money, or lack of sex.

CHAPTER 6

GREEN

Figure It Out

"Information, exploration, and analysis"

I love to solve problems and create new ideas. I need freedom to explore, to learn, to experiment, and to gather information and knowledge.

I need time to think and analyze before I make a decision. Getting at the truth isn't easy. It's hard to get hold of. The facts won't put up with any foolishness. There are lots of possible answers to any question. I am very curious, and I need my independence in order to understand.

I like to learn about the things that interest me, and I am interested in lots of things. I don't like to be told what to do or to think about. I don't like or trust authority unless it really proves itself. I don't like to do the same things over and over again. I like to create and move on, letting others handle the details.

I am more comfortable with ideas and things than I am with feelings and relationships. I want people to appreciate my special contribution to the world. I have strong feelings and I care about what other people feel, but I prefer not to talk about it too much.

Green. What the Greeks called the phlegmatic temperament. What the Yup'ik describe as spirit acting through thought.

In all the trainings that I have done, Greens have nearly always been in the minority. Whatever the actual proportion may be, Greens are unique and special, and often alone among the other Colors.

Greens lead with the power of the thinking mind, approaching all situations with skepticism, seeking new ideas, concepts, designs, and understandings, and relying first, last, and always on their own analysis.

If the Green reader has read this far in this book, it is quite certain that he or she has raised many objections, counterarguments, and skeptical analyses of what is being said. For many Greens, the whole idea of Colors will have seemed overly simplistic, unscientific, and confining.

If the Green reader's interest has been held, it may well be because this idea of Colors has an interesting background with its roots in the Greeks and its relation to Native culture. Or the idea of the types may have sparked an interest, promising a new mental model for analysis and understanding, a new power of comprehension. Greens like powerful models.

One thing is for sure. Whether attending a training or reading this book, Greens doubt everything. If something doesn't make sense to them, they will not just ignore it and go on as if nothing is wrong. They may speak out or raise a challenge. Or they may hold their peace and turn inward. They may close the book or get up and leave the meeting. Depending on their interests and what they want in the situation, they will make up their own minds and act accordingly.

Greens operate based on the evidence. Just the facts, ma'am. They aren't swayed by Blues' personal sentiments or enthusiasm. They mistrust elegant Gold appearances, glossy presentations, and traditional ideas. They will refuse to be caught up in Orange action for its own sake. For Green, it's always a matter of "Let's think this thing over."

Thus, personal integrity and independent analysis are basic keys to understanding extreme Greens. They don't have to have genius-level intelligence. They may have traveled some quite different, independent, nonconformist path in life.

Sometimes Greens' intelligence is overlooked by important people in their lives. On close inspection, it usually turns out that they have been underestimated due to their slow, patient, careful analysis, their refusal to rush to judgment, their unwillingness to give quick and easy answers, and their refusal to simply conform to the prevailing ideas of the people around them.

Greens are interested in applying knowledge: prediction and control, elegant design, problem solving, and dealing skillfully with complexity. They love to feel ingenious, to be experts in everything, to create solutions through their accumulated know-how. Their sexuality partakes of this same intense exploratory quality. Sex is full of curiosity for Greens. Once past the barriers of their overall reserved nature, sexuality is a broad landscape to be explored and enjoyed. It can be a game or a serious expression of deep meaning, but either way, it will be full of experimentation and an opportunity for a kind of vulnerability that many Greens don't find in other areas of life.

But they are even more deeply interested in knowledge and analysis for its own sake. They want to be known as truly complex individuals with great analytic ability. The exercise of intelligence itself, more than its practical application, has the most meaning. "I think, therefore I am," is a good theme for Greens.

Greens prefer to think a thing over rather than to decide about it or arrive at final conclusions. They enjoy looking at a problem afresh each time it is encountered. They like to set aside old approaches, look for a new perspective, a clever insight, an underlying principle, a novel approach, a different outcome.

One unique and recognizable thing about Greens is their hatred of repetition and redundancy. Sometimes it seems almost comical how averse a Green will be to repeating something, or to having to hear it a second time. Green wants it terse, compact, and to the point. "Do not imply that I am stupid by telling me something a second time." "What's the matter, weren't you listening? I already told you once."

Greens doubt their own past conclusions as much as they doubt the ideas of others. Very self-critical, Greens are not personally defensive about their ideas. They are eager for self-improvement and they simply follow knowledge and ideas wherever they lead, even if the ideas contradict what was thought yesterday or ten minutes ago. If someone shows them a real error in their thinking or a truly convincing new idea, the past is left behind easily.

This easy, honest intellectual movement breaks down, however, when Greens feel inferior, inadequate, or out of their depth. At these times, a brittle defensiveness may come into play. Greens are deathly afraid of appearing stupid and inadequate or of actually discovering for themselves that they don't know everything about everything. Fear of humiliation is powerful for Greens.

This constant, here-and-now cogitation sometimes gives the very Green a particularly recognizable appearance: a look of preoccupation sometimes bordering on bewilderment that goes along with a grasping about among a lot of ideas. This highly intellectual, analytical person often seems picky and perfectionist, a bit tense and irritable, especially as ideas are colliding and confusion threatens.

Very Green people can be recognized by their interests. The eccentric, absentminded professor of mathematical linguistics; the librarian specializing in North African topographical maps; the expert statistical theoretician relating the rise and fall of baseball batting averages over the last fifty years to the materials and construction of the ball; the adolescent who knows the inside of Dungeons and Dragons or the motherboard of the computer or the levels of Doom as well as most of us know our address and phone number; the six-year-old with the extensive collection of insect larvae organized by species . . . all are examples of the special worlds of information and knowledge that are created and inhabited by Greens.

The everyday social world can be a real nuisance for Greens. They don't enjoy small talk. They often find that others don't stay with them long enough to relate to their complex interests. The teacher doesn't wait for the answer to her question. She may not even understand her own question as well as the Green does. It is one of a Green's toughest challenges that teachers, parents, and the other Colors tend to drift away while the Green is working the way through a maze of interesting and thoughtful information. Greens are at risk of becoming isolated and eccentric.

In addition, when Greens are out of sorts, they are quite capable of becoming acid-tongued, insolent, and arrogant. When others complain about their attitude or criticize their ideas, they may respond with a sarcastic and condescending smile.

Greens love riddles, mental tricks and games, paradoxes, satire, clever repartee, and intricate intellectual exercises of all kinds, and they enjoy demonstrating their mental power to others. This sometimes makes others feel uncomfortable and on their guard.

Greens can also be rather ruthless when the logic demands it. They will do what's required without much attention to feelings or traditional ways. They often appear puzzled and more than a little irritated when Blues and Golds resist their logic with some nonsense about feelings or about preserving the old ways.

Like Blues, Greens are very inward people. Their feelings run very deep, and they take them very seriously. But for Greens, talking about feelings seems false and contrived. After all, words and feelings are two different things. Talk is not feeling. Greens often say that all the talk about feelings is artificial. It cheapens the feelings. On the other hand, since their feelings are so deep and often unexpressed, Greens are at risk of being seen as cold, distant, uninvolved, and uncaring, even when they care deeply.

Greens contribute a very valuable emotional coolness and deliberateness in situations and relationships. They are not much moved by the subtle emotional messages that people send out with body language and voice tones. If it's not explicit, it gets no attention. There may be an underlying refusal on the part of the Green to be manipulated by these little pressures and emotional subtleties. Greens often see these messages as sneaky, manipulative power games—emotional blackmail—and Greens are not fools to be pushed around in these ways.

On a really excellent, perfect day, a Green has the chance to keep a cool head in a crisis, to bring encyclopedic knowledge to bear on the situation, to weigh up the facts and the options, to design and construct a brilliant, realistic, and effective plan, to consult while others carry out the plan successfully (no tedious effort required of the Green), to save the day, and then humbly and modestly to receive due praise and appreciation from the others for his or her brilliance. For a Green, this is as good as it gets.

Green Dislikes

Greens depend on the integrity of their own autonomous thinking process and the free actions that grow out of it. Some of their deep dislikes tend to be organized around situations that violate rationality and integrity—events that throw their hard-won analyses into disarray.

Illogic and irrationality are among the deepest dislikes for Green. Greens often report that the people around them seem "stupid"—that is, that these people do not think things through until they arrive at logical conclusions that will guide their actions.

Greens gather information, analyze it, and base their actions on the analysis. It is hard for them to understand that others don't necessarily operate this way. The Gold going along by tradition and precedent; the Blue following the lead of feelings and relationships; the Orange acting and then figuring it out later . . . all of these other approaches seem to be illogical, confusing, and ultimately doomed to the deliberate, thoughtful Green.

Greens are not easy in social situations. Most social interaction seems to them to be useless, illogical, and chaotic. They hate prejudice, injustice, unfairness, irrationality, thoughtlessness, stupidity, and overemotionalism . . . in other words, gossip and small talk.

When they are thoroughly disgusted, they tend to drag their feet and become noncompliant. They engage in put-downs and show their scorn for the people and things that have upset them. They often withdraw into a sense of superiority. Their sarcasm is a wonder to behold, and they are masters of the silent treatment.

Redundancy, sloppy thinking, oversimplifying, and mechanical repetition of old ideas will drive a Green from the room. Authoritarian control, intimidation, rigidity, and know-it-alls (particularly those who disagree with them) are great bugaboos. Distractions, time pressure, rote tasks, and nonsense schedules will send a Green looking for another job.

CHAPTER 7

Troubles

Each of the Colors has its own special troubles. Carried to its extreme, each Color has some serious drawbacks and pitfalls. It's a good thing that all the Colors coexist, so that they can check and complement one another. Each Color is often good medicine for the extremes of the others. When there is love, respect, understanding, and communication, we can all help each other get through the worst of our muddles.

GOLD TROUBLES

Golds are usually pretty successful. Their organization, their commitment, and the value they place on accomplishment usually pay off. Still, there are some common difficulties that plague them.

In troubled families, Golds are often stretched to the limit trying to keep things together. It may be Grandma struggling to get the kids on the right track, trying to save marriages, and keep a roof over everybody's head. It may be a child trying to keep peace in the parents' marriage or parenting an irresponsible adult. Wherever the Gold is positioned in the troubled family, he or she will be working hard, and often exhausted and near the breaking point.

Overload and exhaustion are common pitfalls for Golds. “If no one else is doing it, I will have to,” is a common Gold lament. Just as in a troubled family, Golds will struggle to keep a troubled organization afloat, and again the stress and strain will take their toll.

In addition to these difficulties, extreme Golds are subject to various behavior patterns that can be self-defeating and can alienate other people. Their commitment to organization and structure can turn into rigidity. They may become highly judgmental and negative toward others. They may become completely authoritarian and uncompromising. “My way or the highway” may become their motto.

The flip side of authoritarianism is blind following, and this is a common problem when Gold becomes too Gold. Authority is to be respected and obeyed, and this is true whether I am the sheep or the shepherd. Golds can fall into an unquestioning good-soldier mentality, following orders, forgetting to question, surrendering their own independent judgment, and giving all to the cause.

Golds are prone to anxiety and endless hand-wringing. Worry may never leave them. Holidays may be impossible. Worse yet, ambitious vacations may turn into harder work than work. They are also inclined to complaining and self-pity, which is often pretty well justified considering how hard they're working and how little gratitude they get.

Fatigue may become exhaustion. Hypochondria may set in, and real physical complaints may not be far behind. Both Golds and Blues tend to convert life stress into illness or psychosomatic problems. Their sex lives may suffer from accumulated resentments, becoming another of the burdens they carry instead of a release and relief.

Golds need Oranges around. Oranges are frequently irritating to Golds, but they do insist on play, on spontaneity, and on generally "lightening up!" This is a good counterbalance to Gold's tendency toward all work and no play. Golds need Blues as well. Blues offer inspiration and sympathy, and liven up the heart. And they need Greens to question, to be skeptical, to provide alternatives, and to balance Golds' reliance upon precedent and authority.

But above all, Golds need help getting the work done. It is undeniable that the other Colors *all* are happy to let the drudgery fall to the super-responsible Golds. If the Oranges, Blues, and Greens know what's good for them, they will give loving care to the Golds.

BLUE TROUBLES

The deepest troubles for Blues come from the power of their emotions, the depth of their personal sensitivity in relationships, their dreaminess, and sometimes from a kind of self-absorbed narcissism. At the extreme, they are prone to deep anxiety, serious depression, and emotional explosiveness.

Distress in social situations may become almost unbearable. Conflict, rejection, and criticism are very painful, and Blues lose confidence in themselves easily. When things are tough, Blues will often become withdrawn and sulky. Emotional blackmail and passive aggression often come easier for Blues than direct confrontation of issues.

For all their commitment to honesty and authenticity, Blues will lie. They tend to be masters of the little white lie that saves face or avoids emotional unpleasantness. They will lie to save face or cover up their own shortcomings as well. Failure as a person is so painful to Blues that denial and keeping up appearances may seem like the only way out.

Trouble in romantic relationships can be all-consuming. Blues always say that they would rather have a broken arm than a broken heart. When asked to explain, the answer is always the same. The broken arm will heal. The broken heart will hurt forever. Breaking off a bad relationship, like all forms of loss and separation, may be just too hard. Blues often find themselves locked into unhappy situations because it is so hard to say no or to say good-bye. Their sexuality is inextricably entwined with their overall emotional state and may become simply impossible when the life of the heart is out of kilter. On the other hand, illegitimate sexual acting out also may occur, rooted in the depths of loneliness, a sense of powerlessness, and/or self-isolation.

Blues are often dreamy and distracted, living out fantasies while the practical realities tumble down around them. They may have a hard time setting limits, meeting deadlines, getting motivated to carry out their responsibilities.

The demand for self-actualization and self-expression can lead Blues to serious frustrations and overexcitement. They are easily caught up in outlandish belief systems, and they may act out a messianic zeal for whatever happens to be their current enthusiasm. They are also prone to dilettantism, sampling many and various interests and activities, but mastering none.

When Blues are cornered, or when they finally feel justified in their anger, they may be quite emotionally explosive, confrontive, even violent.

Blues can profit greatly from the presence of the other Colors. Gold helps with a firm grasp on practical reality and the ability to

bring stability and order. Orange helps with a light heart and emotional resiliency. Green brings calm rationality, pragmatism, and clear boundaries. All of these can be a great help to the overwrought Blue.

ORANGE TROUBLES

Oranges often get a lot of heat in life. They are criticized, called immature, lazy (which they are *not*), hyperactive, careless, noisy, and so on. Concerned or hostile Golds are after them about risk and disorder. Unfriendly Blues are after them about insensitivity. Unhappy Greens treat them as thoughtless and superficial. Once mighty warriors, hunters, sailors, or respected farmers, mechanics, and artisans, Oranges have a much narrower field of play in the modern world.

Most Oranges rise above all this. They get enough love, enough respect, enough opportunity, enough room to move, and they get along just fine. In fact, they often excel. They may leave school early and never read a book, but they will always be skillful, and they will find ways for that skill to pay off for them.

Some Oranges are not so fortunate, and when Oranges are unhappy, resentful, and rebellious, they act out, they lie, they drop out of school, they run away. They may become rude and defiant in school, in the workplace, in the family, and on the street.

It may become a badge of honor to break laws and rules. Their own lack of respect for comfortable hypocrites and petty tyrants may seem to justify an outlaw lifestyle, or various activities right on the edge of legality or respectability. Lying, cheating, and stealing may become a way of life. Physical aggression may be part of it as well. Overly aggressive sexuality or violation of sexual taboos is not uncommon in stressed-out or unsocialized Oranges who are seeking release for some mighty intense physical demands.

Extreme Oranges are usually looking for the buzz. They tend to prefer stimulants, seeking to heighten their excitement, eliminate fear and anxiety, and reach maximum, ultra-maximum, super-ultra-maximum, radically, devastatingly ultra-super-ultra-maximum intensity, and all this just preparing to *really* go for it the next time around.

Oranges are adventurers and risk takers. Bungee jumping, skydiving, hang gliding . . . pretty soon they are all passé and some new thrill must be found. "Been there, done that" is a common Orange complaint. "No fear!" is an Orange motto.

Oranges are hard to rein in once they have really slipped the leash. They must be approached largely on their own terms: directly, strongly, and often physically. They are not likely to be moved by Blue's appeals to sympathy, by Gold's lectures on order and responsibility, or by Green's arguments and analyses. In the end a change must appear to them to be in their own best interest, and it is on those terms that they must be approached.

Any or all of the offerings from the other Colors *will* be helpful if and when the Orange decides to make a change. But it is no good trying to turn an Orange into a Gold, a Blue, or a Green. Life will always be an adventure for Oranges, and they will keep it lively for the people around them as well.

GREEN TROUBLES

Greens' most serious troubles involve isolation and the power of emotions. Social interaction is never easy for Greens. In extreme situations, they can become seriously disconnected from others. They may have a difficult time finding their way back in.

Greens are well able to build their own world of information and imagination. In the most serious circumstances, they may simply go and live in their inner world. Children and youths may withdraw into comic books, Dungeons and Dragons, the whole world of virtual reality and video games. Adults may disappear into the Internet or into any number of other complex and isolated pathways.

Greens are prone to disgust and cynicism toward their fellow human beings. They may tend to write people off. They are also very vulnerable to feeling rejected, feeling odd, feeling like an outsider. In addition, they may have strong feelings of superiority toward a world that doesn't understand or respect their intelligence, and this superiority may lead them to snobbishness or to strange and eccentric behavior. The search for power can lead troubled Greens down some very unpleasant paths.

On the other hand, Greens are also vulnerable to feelings of inadequacy when they can't comprehend a situation, when they don't know enough, or when they simply don't have the capacity to measure up to their own standards. Feelings of humiliation are deadly to Greens, and they will go to any length to avoid them.

Greens are never easy with emotions. When feelings do well up and come to the surface, Greens sometimes feel overwhelmed and helpless. A flood of feeling can sometimes wash away the power of the intellect to manage things. Deep confusion often results, and it may seem like drowning or like losing all control.

Greens are often prone to indecisiveness in the face of the sheer volume of the information that they possess. Their perfectionism may be overwhelmed by the complexity of a situation.

Their performance anxiety may prevent action and decision. They may try to "baffle them with bull*!#." Or they may become paralyzed, noncompliant, uncooperative, and uncommunicative.

The most common serious difficulty faced by Greens is that others may come to think they are cold and uncaring. This can be a deep wound for a Green, who really cares very deeply. It's the expression that gets in the way. Talk is cheap to a Green. Worse yet, it seems to cheapen the real depth of authentic feelings. One of Greens' worst fears is that no one will ever know how much they really care.

Greens need the support and feedback of the other Colors. Blues can help them to cope with the sea of feelings. Golds can help to bring them back to the concrete world of duty, responsibility, time, and commitment. Oranges, as always, can help them to lighten up, to laugh, to get tough, and to get back on the horse and ride.

CHAPTER 8

Relationships

When Colors Meet Each Other

Richard was a handsome fireball of a salesman with an eye for the uniqueness of a product and a preference for the special quirk, the exotic material, the nifty detail that showed the artisan's genius. He was also an incorrigible flirt from the word *go.* In addition, he was always on the lookout for the really big deal—the deal that, after showing great promise, usually collapsed in a pile of broken dreams. His life had seen a long series of relationships, a couple of broken marriages, and a current marriage that looked like it was going on the rocks, too.

Jeanne, Richard's wife, was a quiet, attractive brunette with special skills at organization and personal relations. She was a working mother, a longtime office manager with a flawless work record. She loved her home and her children and wished for a quiet life. Her children were leaving the nest, and Jeanne was faced with the question of whether she wanted to spend the rest of her life with Richard. She was pretty tired of the strain.

Richard and Jeanne spent many hours deep in tiresome repetition of their age-old struggle to change each other. To Jeanne, Richard was immature, insensitive, and irresponsible, and she felt pain in her heart at what she saw as his lack of caring. Her reading of self-help books led her to hold him up to an image of "the perfect modern man" that was miles from who and what Richard was. To Richard, Jeanne was nagging, dependent, and just too darn sensitive about every little thing. He had been raised in a traditional male household where his father had ruled the roost and brooked no opposition from "the females."

The funny thing was, they really loved one another. In a strange way, it was exactly the things Jeanne criticized in Richard that she loved . . . his spontaneity, his wit, his fearlessness, not to mention his strong, attractive, energetic body. She even enjoyed it that other women found him attractive. The reverse was true for Richard. He loved the sense of peace that he felt when he was with Jeanne. He loved her grace, her delicacy, and her refinement. And above all, he loved her love for him!

One day, Richard's company brought in a Colors trainer to teach selling skills based on the natural differences among customers. The trainer also talked about how the different personalities made different kinds of salespeople. At one point, Richard found himself sitting in a group of people who had identified themselves as Orange. He recognized himself to some degree in every one of them. He enjoyed hearing the trainer describe him and his fellows as a normal, natural, and much-needed segment of the population instead of as a bunch of men and women who never grew up.

As the session went on, he found himself looking across the room at another group of people who had identified themselves as Blue. Suddenly he realized that he could hear Jeanne's voice in every word they spoke: in their wishes and hopes, in their dreams and fears, in their values and needs. He felt the old feeling of love and tenderness rise up inside, and decided then and there to share the Colors experience with Jeanne.

By the time Richard had arranged for Jeanne to join him at a Colors seminar, there were already major changes in their relationship. Richard's views had already begun to change, and he'd used the Colors materials to help Jeanne understand what he had been learning about. They had talked over the differences in their backgrounds, but above all, they had begun to realize that their basic differences were natural, that their personality differences were normal, and that there was nothing wrong with either of them! This realization made all the difference. The pattern of bickering was broken. Evenings of cold silence were replaced by romantic evenings of love and mutual exploration. The children leaving home was no longer a terror for Jeanne. She actually looked forward to the nights when the kids were "sleeping over" with friends, now that she enjoyed "sleeping over" with her husband again. Richard began to understand the way it hurt Jeanne when he was too openly flirtatious, and he found he could let some of that go.

When Richard and Jeanne came to the next seminar, it was plain for all to see that they were discovering each other all over again like a couple of newlyweds. Their marriage is still going strong to this day, more than ten years later.

It has been said that "life is relationship." So what happens when two people's Colors meet? When we study the Colors, we can learn a lot about how we are going to get along with others. Let's turn our attention to mapping out the Colors relationships, discovering where our tensions and conflicts will pop up and what the various Colors have in common with one another. Let's look together at how the relationship will actually work.

Can we know in advance which pairs will be happy and successful and which will not? Can we say which Color makes the right partner for each other Color? Unfortunately—or perhaps fortunately—it's not quite as easy as that. Though we might wish that there were some simple key to matching Colors successfully, there are no cut-and-dried answers. Even two people of the very same Color can get seriously crosswise with each other or bring out shared weaknesses in one another that can spiral into real problems.

As I have traveled around the country meeting thousands of people in Colors seminars, I have seen each of the six possible Colors pairs and the four same-Color couples represented by happy and successful marriages, healthy working relationships, solid and loving parent–child relationships, and so on. When I ask people how many are the same Color as their partners, almost no hands go up. When I ask how many are with someone of different Color than themselves, more than 90 percent of the hands go up . . . every time. It is clear that the differences attract each other and that many factors besides temperament bring people together, though many couples share the same basic Color.

It appears to me that sex is a wild card in the coming together of the Colors in couples. I suspect that this helps nature create a rich and varied gene pool. The Colors intrigue each other. They also complement each other with offsetting strengths and values. The key is in getting along. In courtship, however, we don't always show our "true colors." We play up the things that the other person seems to like and play down the rest of our stuff. Once committed to one another in marriage, we gradually relax into our natural ways of being. This image management is natural and human. It has gone on from time out of mind. But how much better it would be to enter into long-term relationships with a realistic understanding of one another, based on the knowledge that all the Colors are good and necessary and that we will always have to adjust to our differences.

We can observe that some matches are more difficult than others, but we can only understand this when we look closely at the specific profiles of the people involved. Most obviously, if my highest Color is your lowest Color, we will nearly always have difficulties. If I am very Gold and have little Orange to speak of, while you are all Orange with little or no Gold, we are likely to rub each other the wrong way a lot. Love and acceptance will have their work cut out for them. You will be jumping in headfirst while I am still reading the NO LIFEGUARD sign, day in and day out. I'll be planning for retirement while you're having your fun, wanting to spend the money now! At the same time, our other Colors, Green and Blue in this example, will play a role between us, sometimes helping, sometimes throwing in a monkey wrench.

There is no one kind of successful relationship. For some of us in some relationships, we do not need a great deal of intimacy and caring. We may only need to be businesslike and effective, or independent and mutually supportive. This is certainly true in most business and professional relationships. Mutual acceptance and support are important in these relationships for them to be successful in their purposes. Many quite successful marriages are based on independent lifestyles that come together for purposes of parenting, coordination of financial or business interests, family alliances, management of property, and so forth. Even sex may or may not be a part of the marriage contract. Gold and Green, particularly, may find themselves in very businesslike marriages or may intentionally seek them out. When we really understand natural human differences, we see that relationships can take a nearly infinite variety of forms.

Love is not a Color. In the Eye of Awareness, the Yup'ik symbol mentioned in the second chapter, the center of the circle is an open spiritual space, free of color. It is the energy that transcends all four Colors. When we have this loving energy—that is, when we have open affection, understanding, respect, and acceptance in our hearts—then the natural differences among our Colors will be a source of shared strength, of mutual challenge, of enrichment and variety in our lives. Here in our center, affection, understanding, respect, and acceptance are attitudes that we all can share, whatever our Color. Our friend, lover, spouse, workmate, parent, or child will bring richness to our lives, a richness that can outweigh the various frustrations that are inevitable when our differences are strong.

GOLD IN RELATIONSHIPS

So, my Gold friend, how are you doing with the important responsibilities and burdens you are carrying? Are you on your own? Are you surrounded by the other Colors or do you have some other fairly strong Golds around helping you carry things? Are you struggling to keep the ship afloat pretty much on your own, pursuing your goals and the good of the community? For you, relationships are usually about trying to get the other Colors to pitch in, to do some work—and about trying to get them to do it right! Sometimes it's better for you to just do the task yourself. You'll have to clean up the mess later anyway, if you delegate it.

The other Colors are glad you're there. They will usually admit how much they depend upon you. You are usually so good at working your fingers to the bone, and doing it without letting others know how much stress you're feeling, that they forget how much they need you. I think you would be wise to remind them in concrete terms, and do so fairly often. Take a sick day once in a while just on general principles. This will help others remember. If you build in some reminders for them before your resentment builds up too much, they might even pitch in and help. But when your hurt and resentment mount up and make you sulky and sour, the other Colors will run and hide—or else they will counterattack. Relationships will suffer.

You have very high standards of behavior, of belief, and of appearances. These standards are an important part of your contribution to the community of strengths represented by the Colors. You work hard to meet these standards, and you may expect that you can encourage others to do so as well. This turns out to be a doubtful proposition, however. The other Colors cannot simply conform to your standards any more than you could give them up. Look for their strengths and build standards for them that match what they can do. When they are doing the best at what comes naturally to them, they will be better able to meet your expectations, and they will also be making their best contribution to whatever it is that needs doing.

Gold and Gold

Let's suppose a new person comes into your life. You notice that the first thing they do is to look around and find out what it is that's important to you, what important burdens you are carrying. You notice that they respect your values and priorities. Once they understand what's really important to you, they set about helping in some practical way if they can. They don't offer reassuring hugs. They don't propose some sort of fun or restful escape. They don't offer a ten-page analysis of the situation and tell you what to do about it. They simply, carefully, and skillfully set about being helpful in getting the job done, and done right.

Is it a miracle? No, it's just another Gold who has taken a genuine interest in you. They will follow up on the helpfulness with spontaneous acts of generosity and thoughtful gifts. If it's courtship, it will be solid and enjoyable. If it's a new work relationship, it will be really helpful. In addition, the person will put on their best appearance for you or for your customers or colleagues. They'll be on time for things. If they are late, it won't be because they were goofing around. It will be because of other serious commitments that they are honoring, and this may be the first hint of where difficulties can arise between you.

So much will be right for you about this Gold person. At the same time, however, if they have other commitments—and chances are they will—you will find that they are sometimes caught between them, and you may not always come first in line for time and attention. Especially after the honeymoon is over. In a marriage, you can expect that their loyalty to their family of origin will be as strong as yours, and you know how strong that is.

Along the same lines, if you have differences of opinion about important values or social issues, work approaches on the job, religious differences, parenting, sexuality, or other behavioral differences at home, your partner will be just as stubborn as you are. Here comes "my way or the highway," which is especially strong with other Golds.

With a Gold spouse, you will share the strong-willed, traditional lifestyle and a firm and steady pace of living. Unless one of you craves a bit more spice, a more adventuresome sexuality, a bit more sentiment, or a bit more intellectual stimulation, Gold and Gold will get along well. The checkbook will always balance. The yard will be mowed. The family, both nuclear and extended, will be remembered and cared for. Surprises will be kept to a minimum.

Gold and Blue

Here's someone who will join you in keeping the peace. They will do it for very different reasons than yours. For them, emotional harmony is the highest goal in relationships. They avoid emotional pain wherever possible . . . both in themselves and in others. You, on the other hand, keep the peace as part of your duty to the success and stability of the family or work group. Between the two of you, the people around you will be taken care of.

You'll know the Blues by the tone of sympathy they bring to your conversations, especially when they find out how hard you are working, the stress you are under. The Blue will be more likely at first to give you a hug or put flowers on your desk than to pitch right in with the work itself. You will find them to be most concerned with the state of your heart—your emotional heart, that is. "How are you feeling?" "How do you feel about it?" "How does this feel?" are the questions most often asked by Blues. They live in their feelings, and they will look to your feelings as the key to your relationship. If you are happy with them, it won't matter to them that quarterly profits are down, that the well has run dry, or that there's nothing in the refrigerator for dinner.

You will find that the Blues are attracted to the same social settings as you. If you are working in a service industry, a social-service agency, or an elementary school, there you'll find Blues on every side, along with other Golds. Once again, they are there out of the needs of their hearts, while you are there out of a duty to the community. They will be focused on the interpersonal process and relationships. You will be getting the job done. In a marriage, they will be looking for expressions of feelings. They want to hear "I love you" several times a day, whereas you would be content with some help around the house, remembered birthdays and special occasions, and a good social impression as a solid couple. They will want sex to be full of romantic words and gestures of assurance that you really care, and in return they will be deeply generous and inventive in their lovemaking. For you, it must fit into a busy schedule, and nothing too out of the ordinary.

You will share a deep concern for the children, a deep sense of parental responsibility. For you, this will show itself in the practical care you give, the safe environment you provide, the expectations you insist upon. Love will be shown by all the things you do and give. For the Blue, much more will be expressed in words, emotional expressions, and gestures of affection. If you are facing a life-threatening surgery, you will want the children to know where their next meal is coming from. The Blue will want them to know they are loved. They will want to pass on a last word or two of wisdom, while you're making sure they know where the will is and who gets Grandfather's pocket watch.

You will find the Blue a bit hard to understand when it comes to what they call *authenticity* or some such word. You will be carrying on quite successfully in a certain course of action when suddenly the Blue will bail out or call a halt because it "doesn't fit," or "it's just not me!" When you dig a little deeper, you'll find that the success they're seeking isn't really much about money, security, or recognition, but about some sort of personal realization or development that's hard as heck to figure out. All you can do is love or tolerate it. It goes with the package. The good news is that the Blue will generally love and look out for the best in you, celebrate your happiness along with all your other lovely emotions, empathize with your sorrows and feelings of failure, and let you off your own hook when it comes to your high standards.

Gold and Orange

Look out! Here comes some excitement. There's an old Chinese curse that goes, "May you live in interesting times." For the Orange, this is no curse. It's what they hope for every day. I knew a strong Orange in high school who used to sit in math class looking out the window and wishing and hoping that the butte south of town would erupt just for the sheer fun of it (and so that school would let out!).

You can feel the energy when an Orange walks into the room. Except for the few quiet Oranges, their bodies are almost never still. They love fast-paced action and lots of stimulation. They can work with the radio on, study while pedaling an exercise bike or jogging on a treadmill. They are deeply independent in action, automatically resisting authority unless it squares with where they want to go anyway.

If you meet an Orange with a strong Gold second Color, they will show you how to be Gold with energy and enthusiasm, how to make work a game, to compete with yourself and others just to make it interesting. Your love life won't involve just quiet intimacies and thoughtful gifts; rather, the Orange will bring impulsive expressions of affection and fun and a vigorous sexuality. They may forget your anniversary, but every day will have the quality of a celebration.

When it comes to loyalty, they will be tempted when they are away from you to love the one they're with. Depending upon circumstances, and depending upon the strength of their other Colors, they may or may not succumb. I have known Golds who had open-marriage agreements with their spouses, but for most Golds, this loyalty issue will be one hard thing about pairing up with an Orange. Really, it's more about living up to commitments and agreements than about loyalty per se. Orange lives in the here and now, and words that were spoken weeks, months, or years ago seem pretty far away when the moment is full of new opportunities.

Oranges are very nonjudgmental. "Live and let live" is more natural to them than "my way or the highway." Still, they very much share your Gold concrete practicality. They love money and the things it can buy, though they want to spend it now while you might want to save it for the future. They love good appearances, though their ideas about fashion may be a bit more flamboyant than yours . . . maybe more than a bit. They like the fresh and new where you prefer the tried and true.

As a couple, you will have the energy and the organization to do whatever you put your minds to. There will probably be some head-butting along the way, but if the two of you understand these differences and see the value of your individual contributions, the sky's the limit for accomplishment.

Gold and Green

This is where things get serious. When Gold and Green are attracted to each other, it is usually around a very businesslike approach to life. Unless Orange is also strong in one or both, Green and Gold combine talents for serious purposes. Neither you nor the Green is much for devil-may-care, kick-off-your-shoes fun and games, unless you are in the right place at the right time, unless you have made sure that the situation is safe, the curtains are drawn, and business is buttoned down tight.

Once again, depending upon the mix of your other Colors, you and your Green partner are not inclined to indulge in romantic nonsense. You have deeper satisfactions. Real accomplishment. Quality in what you do, what you think, what you believe. Down-to-earth matters. Achievement. Freedom from foolishness, childishness, error. Perfection is a high goal. It involves commitment and ability. Between you, you and your Green partner may just have what it takes to reach it. But you both know that your performance can always be improved upon.

If you are attracted to a serious Green, the chances are that you are also attracted to the toughest, most difficult and exacting sort of work and activities. You may be in the professions with lives depending upon you. You may be practicing skills that require utmost dedication and constant work. Your Green partner will either join you in that work, contributing their powerful analytical intelligence, or they will be pursuing similar interests of their own. This may result in your leading parallel lives, respecting one another's endeavors, meeting outside of work for times of mutual appreciation, rest, and the joy that comes from someone understanding your accomplishments.

Difficulties will arise when the Green's endless analysis begins to impair your demand for action and productivity. For them, there simply can never be enough data, and the latest fact uncovered can turn an entire plan right on its head. Deadlines may seem meaningless as the Green follows the pace of the information instead of the pace of the project.

At home, the Green spouse may fail to take notice of the detail work involved in maintaining the household. Other interests occupy them, and these other interests may look to you like "just sitting around" as they spend their time reading, watching the latest documentary or film on TV, or pursuing quiet hobbies in the workshop, while you maintain the wardrobe and environment, or try to keep up appearances for the neighbors. Green pays little attention to appearances. It's the quality of the content that matters to them. Appearances seem superficial, and people who focus on appearances may seem shallow to the intellectual Green.

Green brings an inventiveness and exploratory quality to sex. Their interests may explore directions that are a bit too unusual for your tastes. Gold and Green is not usually the relationship that sparks fireworks and causes the earth to move. This is the relationship that designs and builds the stable platform from which the fireworks may be fired, and invents and markets the machinery to measure the movements of the earth.

BLUE IN RELATIONSHIPS

It must have been a Blue who said that "life is relationship." As a strong Blue, you may not live entirely for relationships, but whatever you live for, your active, emotional heart will be reacting to relationships pretty much all the time. You'll value justice and abhor injustice. You'll spend much time in sympathy and compassion for the downtrodden, worrying about mistreated children and animals, and wishing the best for underdogs everywhere. Relationships are deeply moving to Blues. They are the source of belonging and the field in which life takes place. They are also the source of most of the pain in your life.

As a Blue, you feel this special sensitivity in all your relationships. You want this sensitivity from others, but many others simply don't share it. You want to bring out the best in everyone you meet and you expect others to share this wish . . . but not everyone does. You take criticism personally, whereas many people thrive on being critical. For a strong Blue, sex is completely wrapped up with emotion, commitment, and romantic love. For many non-Blues, especially Greens and Oranges, sex is just sex—a good time, a release, or a well-deserved reward.

Blue and Blue

When you meet another Blue, there may be a special sharing that takes place. If you have been living with mostly Oranges, Golds, and Greens, it will be a relief to meet someone who shares your Blue feelings. You will find that you have much in common. If you meet as intimate friends or lovers, chances are you will share your dreams, your emotions, your rich fantasy life, and a mutually affirming sexuality. If you meet in a work setting, you will likely share opinions about the culture of your workplace, whether it's people-friendly and caring, or cold, efficient, and hard on employees. You will find that similar things make you angry and other things make both of you happy or sad.

It is a common experience when two Blues are in a relationship that you may reinforce the patterns you have in common, including your difficulties. You may find yourselves spiraling down into a shared depression or gloominess as you discover your agreements about hard and negative things in life. Of course, you may also share and support each other's joys. For better or worse, you will both be likely to give special attention to feelings and emotions. Feelings last a long time for Blues, therefore your past experiences, positive or negative, will have important effects over time.

If you marry a Blue, this mutual reinforcement of feelings will have a major impact on the quality of your marriage. If you are considering marriage, it will be important to pay attention to which way this shared feeling process commonly takes you. Courtship is a time of putting your best foot forward, and Blues are extremely good at adjusting to the wants of others, but you can always find subtle hints of the underlying patterns that may become major elements of your relationship over time.

Blue and Gold

As a Blue, when you meet a Gold, your emotional sensitivity must allow for their emphasis on order and productivity. In a lover, you will be looking for the typical elements of intimacy: gentle touches, quiet moments, deep sharing, loyalty, creativity, and the expression of feelings. These will be the things you try to communicate to the Gold. Golds are often happy to meet Blues in this way. They enjoy sharing these things, especially when the sharing contributes to a successful relationship. That's what Golds want: a successful, solid, orderly, productive relationship.

Golds want to be appreciated for their hard work and their

good qualities, and as a Blue, you are more than willing to give them the recognition for which they are longing. As the relationship settles down for the long term, your Gold partner will live more and more fully in their hardworking, practical style. Some of the delightful moments of intimate sharing and subtle tenderness will tend to fall away as the Gold settles into deeply held values about hard work, productivity, maintaining good appearances, and fulfilling social responsibility.

Your style of following inspiration, of "leading with your heart," and your tendency toward dreaminess will bump into the Gold's practicality and reliance on the past, on precedent and procedure. If you are trying to build a house together, you will bring many innovative ideas, even eccentric ones, while the Gold will be deeply concerned with maintaining an acceptable image in the community.

Your sense of forgiveness and sympathy will clash with the Gold's more conservative morality and tendency to judge people according to traditional standards. Your intimate expressions of love, affection, and appreciation will meet the Gold's style of showing love by giving gifts and doing things for others. They may look for gifts and practical help as evidence of your affection for them while you are sending them great waves of love and affection through your own language and gestures—which they may not understand or appreciate. You may come to feel that their reliance on things and their practicality are really not very romantic; you may even come to doubt an authentic love for you simply because it's expressed in a different way than you're accustomed to.

Unless Gold is a pretty strong influence in you as well, you will have a hard time dealing with their critical nature, their commitment to standards and results, and their impatience with sentimentality. For all these differences, however, you and Gold have much in common. You both value good work and cooperation in the community, helpfulness and order in relationships. If you are working together in a service occupation, you will often find yourselves natural allies—though once again the Gold will be more focused on a well-running organization while you are dedicated to well-served clients. As a couple, you will find yourselves sharing community activities and a genuine concern for the welfare of others.

Obviously, conflict will arise when the Gold's emphasis on duty, roles, appearances, and productivity come up against your emphasis on persons, feelings, emotional harmony, and creativity. When you fight with each other, you will tend to accuse the Gold of being rigid and unfeeling. The Gold will counter that you are overly emotional, romantic, dreamy, naive, and wishy-washy. You will make up when you remember and appreciate your common ground. Service and good relationships often bridge the natural differences between you. Together, you carry tremendous responsibility in the community.

Blue and Orange

When you meet an Orange, there may be an immediate dislike, or there may be a strong attraction. To you as a Blue, the Orange will appear to have a freedom and a sense of fun and creativity that you might dearly love to possess yourself. You may envy this freedom or you may resent it. Either way, as you become closer to one another, there is likely to be a strong reaction between you. Blue and Orange are the nonlinear, right-brain Colors. This means emotion and sensation. Orderly analysis and strict structures do not come naturally to either Color. Feelings run high—but for the Orange, feelings are physical and they are of the moment, here and now. Feelings are simpler for them than they are for you, and they don't last so long. Tomorrow is a new day. Yesterday's argument is past and gone. Whereas for you, yesterday is a live issue. As is last week and ten years ago. The Blue heart has a long memory.

Blues often fall in love with Oranges for their physical grace and emotional freedom. But with Orange, a sting can be waiting. Orange moves easily from relationship to relationship. Good-byes are not difficult. Hellos are natural and comfortable. For you, as we have seen, every good-bye is like a little death, and even something as simple as not being noticed by someone can feel like being cut off and thrown away.

This is the price of Blue loving Orange. Orange will not naturally take care of the Blue's deep sensitivity in relationships. They will forget anniversaries and birthdays. They will be deeply involved in a game or an activity and completely miss your cues that you need their attention, their reassurance, their affection. There is no malice or lack of affection in this, though the Blue tends to see it that way. It is simply that Orange is doing what they are doing at any given moment. Their basic message to all of us is, "Lighten up. Do something. Get back on the horse. You're tougher than you think you are."

It's wonderful when Blue learns the lessons that Oranges are teaching. They can help you find the freedom they enjoy. Their creativity fits in well with yours. It enriches yours and takes it in directions you haven't even thought of, or have been afraid to attempt. They can help you lift your spirits when you're "blue," and Blues are frequently "blue." Oranges are not intimidated by authority or tyrannized by rules and bureaucracy. They can show you how to "just do it" and not always wait around for the approval of some authority figure. They live by the motto "I'd rather be told 'Stop!' than be told 'No!'"—so they boldly and blithely go off in creative directions that, as a Blue, you wouldn't dare.

Orange tends to prefer general camaraderie to quiet intimacy. For the Orange, sex is playful, often even athletic. Those quiet moments with long lingering glances and whispered intimacies are not a necessary part of their sexuality. They live in the body primarily, and sex is about sensation for them. You may find the Orange to be impatient with your need for a certain atmosphere before sex can be enjoyable. As a Blue, you will find that when you are upset about something, especially something in your relationship, sex just isn't the thing for you. In all honesty, Blues are not above withholding sex when they are angry or upset. This is part of Blues' survival strategy in life, which often involves passive-aggressive strategies that make up for their lack of pure, straightforward aggression. For your Orange partner, on the other hand, sex may be just the thing to take their mind off whatever is troubling them . . . or troubling you!

You'll find that for Orange, life is a game, and winning is the best thing of all. They love risk and the excitement of new sensations. Depending upon their second Color, you may find them quite unable to join you in your sensitive concerns for others and for the world. They are strongly independent and take care of their own first. They tend to be impatient with your willingness to sacrifice, because it goes against their deeply held appreciation for individual responsibility and autonomy. They will make an exception, however, when your self-sacrifice works to their benefit. Why look a gift horse in the mouth, eh?

Unless you have some strong Orange in you, you will have a hard time with their impulsiveness, their sensation-seeking, and their inattention to sentiment. As we have seen, Oranges make up a bit more than one-third of the population according to the literature. Only a fraction of these are extremely Orange. As with all potential partners, friends, or associates, the power of the other Colors will soften the impact of their primary Color. Take these things into account when deciding how far you wish to bring Orange into your life. Your creativity and your reliance on things other than cold reason and logic to guide you give you much in common. Your ability to experience real joy and excitement together can offset much that pushes you and Orange apart.

Blue and Green

Green shares with you the inward life. You look inward for guidance from your feelings. Green looks inward to their reason and understanding. Like you, Green is sensitive to input from the outside world, but their sensitivity often leads them to isolate and protect themselves, whereas you may set out to interact with the world and try to make it safe and right. Both of you share an ability to find value in solitary activities and various kinds of meditation.

Greens have a great deal to teach you. They are able to make boundaries in life, whereas for you, life is all one big event, and it usually seems to be all mixed together. Work and home, community and family, religion and daily life . . . everything flows together for you. Green can make compartments, putting work in its place, home in its place, community in its place, and so on. They know how to hold their tongues in situations where you may well blurt out your feelings inappropriately. They know how to say no in situations where you can't seem to keep from saying yes.

You may fall in love with their rationality, their ability to explain, to discover reasons and the logic of situations. Above all, you may admire, even envy, their autonomy. Green is as independent as Orange, if not more so, since Orange seeks out camaraderie. Greens think for themselves, and they are usually not afraid to disagree with others. They tend to put the facts ahead of relationships and are not willing to compromise the data just to keep someone happy or friendly toward them. For you, of course, the hostility of others is painful.

Tension between you and the Green will begin to arise when their logic and their love of problem solving run into your feelings and sensitivities. You will share a sadness, and they'll offer a solution. They will expect the solution to resolve the sadness and will become impatient with you if you would rather stay with the sadness. You will communicate an enthusiasm, and they will toss off a bit of logic or a few facts that completely pop your bubble. You will approach them for an intimate moment and they will turn away into an interest or preoccupation of their own. You will interpret silence as negative. They will see it as neutral or, better yet, a relief. You will look for words of appreciation or of love and affection, and they will be silent, letting their actions speak.

For you, sharing a feeling with someone makes it more real. For the Green, talking about deep feelings may seem to cheapen the feelings, to make them trivial. Greens have a quiet and deliberate emotional style, often seeming quite cool, even cold. Greens' sexuality often has an almost intellectual quality about it, far from the luxurious intimacy and romanticism that you enjoy so much. Greens like sex for its own sake, and for its inventive possibilities. Still, they definitely have some deep feelings. They care. They want to belong. They want to be appreciated. They just don't want to chat about it. Small talk doesn't interest them, and deep sharing is very difficult. This makes for some long silences when you're wanting to talk about everything under the sun.

You will probably be much more social overall than your Green friend, lover, or colleague. When you are seeking out human contact for its own sake, Green is finding ways to avoid having to deal with it. You will need to develop some independent relationships in order to take care of yourself in a marriage to a Green. They will have many independent interests of their own, but socializing probably won't be one of them. Greens can become very controlling and possessive when they are insecure; you may need to assert your social needs while at the same time reassuring them of your loyalty.

Unless you have some pretty strong Green in yourself, you will have a hard time with their tough skeptical nature, their impatience with your dreamy enthusiasms, their coolness and unwillingness to share feelings, and their stubborn independence. On the other hand, you share the inner world in its entirety between you. Blue and Green together can lead lives of deep meaning and spiritual search. While Gold and Orange provide the energy and structure of life, you and your Green partner will deepen the experience.

ORANGE IN RELATIONSHIPS

I'll keep this moving right along, my Orange friend. I know you've got things to do, places to go, people to see. Ah yes, but what people? That's the relationship question. Who are the good work partners, the best lovers? Who is enjoyable in small doses and who is a candidate for the long-term relationship? Are you even thinking about the long term? Are you looking for a life mate or a playmate? Do you want someone who will hit the deck at full speed, or who will at least make zero to sixty in eight seconds or less? Or are you looking for someone who can slow you down a bit, help with the details, keep an eye on the clock, remind you about the bank closing, the taxes coming due? Or maybe you're ready for some romance. Hearts and flowers. Sweet nothings in your ear. Maybe even make a baby or two. Or perhaps it's time in your life to study something, to really learn, to get at the meat of some subject that will take you where you want to go. Who do you want to go with you?

If you're like most Oranges, you're going to value a sense of humor. That means someone who doesn't take themselves or anyone else too seriously. A lot of good Orange humor comes out of a distaste for conceit, for people who are puffed up, who are too high on themselves. These are the folks you may enjoy bringing down a peg, and doing it in a way that shows them that you know something, too. This is probably not a firm basis for a long-term relationship, though it may be good for a few laughs in the short run. At work you may have no choice. You may have to put up with the boss or move on. But in a friend or a lover, you can choose.

To go along with that humor, you probably would appreciate a generally upbeat and active disposition. Not too much gloom and doom. As little whining as possible. Not too much sitting around and introspecting. An unexamined life may not be worth living, but an unlived life isn't worth examining, either. On the other hand, it might be nice to find someone who does enough thinking and reading and so on to carry on a decent conversation. A little wit, for sure. Dull people need not apply.

You might want to get with somebody who specializes in some of the things you aren't attracted to. Balancing the checkbook, for example, and of course contributing something to the bank account. Cleaning house. Keeping the wardrobe in good shape. You like to look sharp, and you like decent surroundings. It's all that upkeep that gets you down. Some people actually don't mind doing it as much as you do. You might be able to strike a deal where you take care of some things you enjoy and they take care of some things you don't. Deal making comes naturally to you, doesn't it? Right along with making life a game and enjoying a good win–win?

Of course, a little style wouldn't hurt, a little flair, a bit of creativity in outlook and presentation. It doesn't have to be Miss America or Mr. Olympia if the style and attitude are there. Casual. Cool. Active. Helpful. Nonjudgmental. Nothing to it. You must meet half a dozen people like that every time you go to the grocery store. *Not!*

You're probably going to want a socially active life. Most Oranges are quite gregarious. You love to chat and play and generally be around other human beings in friendly, low-stakes camaraderie or high-energy competition. For many of you, this group activity bridges easily into having several different romantic partners; from ongoing flirtation and bawdy humor right on into bed. Not so easy for most of the other Colors. Between fear of the consequences, fear of the body, fear of triangles, and just plain fear, the other Colors may actually hold that sexual energy of yours against you. If you're getting into something permanent, you'd better get clear about this issue. Your casual enjoyment may have a way of blowing up in your face down the road.

Getting into work groups and teams, you are a natural cheerleader and a goer/doer from the get-go. The work team needs your humor and excitement, but count on it, they also want more compulsiveness than you're comfortable providing. The clock, the calendar, the policies and procedures manual, the memo, that strong Gold in the next office or acting as crew chief . . . these can all be your friends. Stay on top of them and your relationships will prosper. Try to dodge them or stall them and it rarely works for long. Instead, become a speed reader. Learn touch typing. Make it a competition. Use your quick skills to beat the game on its own terms; ten minutes a day at your speed will put you well ahead of the pack. Then you'll be crew chief. You can do the micromanaging and be a nuisance to everyone else about deadlines and quality benchmarks. Or else work your way into self-employment and hire a Gold to keep the books and manage your schedule.

Orange and Orange

Now, this should be pure fun, right? Somebody just like you. Or are they? First of all, what's their second Color? An Orange/Green can cut you up with sarcasm and a devastating wit. An Orange/Gold has climbed the management ladder with drive, ambition, and an orderly approach and may just leave you in the dust. An Orange/Blue really cares about other people's feelings and may shake a finger at you about how long it's been since you called Mom. So first of all . . . there's Orange and then there's Orange.

Now, maybe they really are just like you. Impatient, fun-loving, living in the here and now. If you've both been loved and cared for and have a healthy respect for yourselves and each other, the sky's the limit. It can be a really great time. Sex will be over the top! Of course, they can't keep track of their bank balance any better than you can. They love to live beyond their means as much as you do. They have the boss or the teacher down on their necks just like you do. They love a clean house but don't love to follow the routine that keeps it that way.

When two Oranges interact, there will often be a pattern of winding up or winding down. Maybe I wind down when you wind down and wind up when you wind up. Maybe the more I wind up, the more you wind down. Maybe the more you wind up, the more I wind down. For example, maybe when my voice gets louder, you tend to get quieter. Or maybe when you get louder, I get louder.

Two Oranges who both wind up can wind up pretty tight. When I get louder and you get louder, too, it can result in some pretty noisy conversation! Or take irritability and quick temper. I snap at you and you snap back and pretty soon, these emotions can wind up into quite a storm. The good news is that for Orange, when the spat is over, it's over. It can be like the sun coming out after a thunderstorm—almost instantaneous relief and the ability to just go on as if nothing ever happened. This is endlessly astonishing to Blues, for whom emotions have long tails.

Orange and Gold

Here is one of the most ancient and common arguments of all: spontaneity versus order, freedom versus rules, entertainment versus earnestness. It is also one of the most ancient of complementarities, a lovely batch of balancing strengths. Orange and Gold are the two concrete, action- and results-oriented Colors. You won't find that Gold partner or colleague spending much time navel-gazing or going in for endless hair-splitting. Action is the order of the day for both of you. Your Gold buddy will bring the map and the flashlight, and you will bring the excitement and the love of risk and adventure. Between you, you just might have what it takes to get the mountain climbed, the jungle mapped, the source of the Nile tracked down.

Of course, all the way up the Nile you'll argue with each other. The Gold will tell you that you are childish and immature. You will counter that they're rigid and uncreative. In return, you will be told to settle down and face facts, to which you will reply that life is too short to settle and that you were the one who had the guts to take on this adventure in the first place. If your Gold partner gets a little pompous and conceited, you will find yourself spontaneously coming up with practical-joke strategies. They will provide the nose in the air, you will provide the banana peel under their shoe. They'll inflate the balloon, you'll provide the pin.

On the other hand, your Gold will sure be good looking, making the best of their assets, showing real care for their appearance. The image won't be flashy, but it will have class. They'll have nice things. Once again, class. They'll be successful, too. They will have done what it takes to be sure that they are. While you have played the angles, exploited your natural talents to the max, and taken every shortcut you could find to get where you are as quickly and painlessly as possible, the Gold will have planned, studied, practiced, met the standards one by one, and earned the paper, the title, or the position. They'll have earned a lot of the things you would love to have.

You and the Gold will share a deep impatience with slow-moving, dreamy, intellectual, and romantic types. Fortunately for you, you and your Gold counterparts make up a substantial majority of the human race at any given time, while the dreamers and analyzers are left in the minority. The good Lord in infinite evolutionary wisdom selects action and energy, Orange and Gold, as primary over the more passive, responsive temperaments, the Blues and the Greens. Still, your Gold partner will probably act more cautiously than you would in most situations. Sex will be more appropriate and constrained. It may well be a Gold driving that poky car ahead of you, the one that just cost you your chance to make it through the intersection on yellow instead of having to take it on red so that you now have to visit with this nice policeman.

Orange and Blue

Whether in work, in friendship, or as a couple, your own active passions will have more appeal than the spectator activities of art appreciation, sports watching, or reading the words of others. Obviously, there are many exceptions to these observations. But what's important in the Orange–Blue relationship will always be some form of spontaneous creativity, an openness to the new, a lack of standard judgments in favor of a gut-level appreciation of anything open, energetic, freewheeling, fresh, passionate, perceptive, whole.

Practicality and concrete order go out the window in favor of the first impression, the quick association, the laugh or the tear; for things done for the fun of it, for the challenge of it, for the excitement of it. The body and its sensations loom large in the Orange–Blue world. The heart and its "rays and pangs" is like a furnace generating power, heat, and emotion at the center of the organism. Physical movement comes out of the musculature and the heart. It is ecstatic and creative just for its own sake. Everything exists for its own sake.

Time is rhythmic and circular for Orange and Blue. The past is judged alongside the present on an equal footing. It has no special authority just because it has stood the test of time. For the Orange, the standards of the past are to be competed with, improved upon . . . always the personal best is out there to be reached for.

The really good news for the Orange about Blue is that Blue really loves passionately. Your Blue partner will appreciate things about you that you don't even know about yourself. They will admire, even envy your freedom, the way you seem to live without pain while they are feeling their own pain and everybody else's. *Passion* is a key word in this relationship. In a work setting, the Blue will want to find ways to feature your skill, talent, and creativity. They may fight with you to get you to be more sensitive to others' feelings, but they are not likely to join forces with the Golds who may want to put a muzzle on you.

In a marriage, Blue loves to love you. As long as there is some romance, some gentleness and intimacy, sex will be good . . . creative and adventuresome. When your Blue partner's out of sorts, however—feeling used or unappreciated, or unhappy about completely unrelated things—sex is not only unpleasant, it's practically impossible. Far from being an enjoyable escape from emotional unpleasantness, sex must come from a positive emotional background or Blue won't play. If they stuff their feelings and go ahead just to please you, the bad energy will accumulate.

When Blues have had enough, they blow big time. "Long fuse, big bang": That's Blue. When they blow, I call it the Samson syndrome. I imagine the Blue standing between two support pillars that hold up the entire temple, their long hair flowing, their rage at injustice cranked up to ten, and suddenly they pull the whole world down around the ears of the gathered multitude. That's the fed-up Blue. And they are especially good at it, since they have an instinct for the jugular. During the buildup phase, they have been protecting your vulnerable points. Now, at rage time, they head straight for them. In addition, Blue feelings don't go away immediately the way your Orange ones do. It's a long time, if ever, before the Blue gets over it—whatever it is.

Orange and Green

Now, here comes somebody who goes places you may never have really explored, like the reference room at the library. You'd be surprised at what they are looking for in there. You probably think they're searching for facts and information about some fourteenth-century monastic order or the essential principle of the solenoid, and they may be doing just that. If you look a little closer, though, you'll discover that what they are really digging out of those musty old tomes is power. In the Green world, whether it's the university, the Mensa study group, the engine repair shop, the vegetable garden, or the stock market, knowledge is power. As an Orange, chances are you share with the Green a love of power. You gather it in order to win in open combat. They gather it to have and to hold and to measure out in careful, strategic doses.

You may well enter into a strategic alliance to fight against having power exerted over you. You won't be told what to do. Green won't be told what to think. Between you, authority figures will have a rough time. You both probably enjoy exercising power, each in your own way. Green likes to keep a low profile with power, and being the boss may require more "bossiness" than the Green enjoys exerting. You, on the other hand, pretty much thrive on the exercise.

You will be more of a team player than the Green, who tends to prefer a more solitary and independent relationship to the group. They enjoy making their input from a little distance and often leave it to others to carry out their insights. The Green becomes a long-distance runner. The Orange likes a nice line of scrimmage.

You will be generally more impetuous than your Green friend or partner. They will prefer to think things through in advance, to anticipate the bumps in the road, to apply just the right leverage at just the right places to get the job done with a minimum of effort and hassle and, above all, a minimum risk of failure or humiliation. Humiliation is what it means to lose, to fail, to make a goof. Looking stupid is just about the ultimate horror to most Greens. They are generally relentless in their analytical criticism of the performance of others, and equally so of their own. Their own failures and humiliations are just about the only places where Greens will turn away from the facts, hiding their errors or putting the best face on them when they can.

Often the Orange spouse will tell me that it's common for their Green partner to "suddenly" decide that they want to move forward on an idea that was proposed to them six months ago. Of course, the Orange had almost forgotten about the darn idea in waiting for a response. Green wheels grind slowly, but they grind exceedingly fine.

Sexually, both of you will have considered open marriage unless your Blue or Gold influences have prevented it. I recommend that you handle this issue aboveboard with one another rather than doing it on the sly. Greens are vulnerable to feeling that they have been made fools of, and you are vulnerable to feeling tricked by the Green's excellent strategies. Better to put it on the table and have some clear agreements. When the agreements are in place and working, the sex will be inventive. The Green will probably take you places you have never thought of before while you provide the rocket fuel that keeps the fire burning.

As work colleagues, you will each have your eye on the prize in your own way. Once again, putting this on the table will prevent misunderstandings and bloodletting. Find the win–wins between you. If there are to be win–lose transactions, let the outside competition take the losses rather than either of the two of you. Competition can be fun, though, as you well know. Greens can enjoy it, too, especially if it gives them a chance to demonstrate their smarts. Nice open competition with well-defined playing fields and some clear rules can generate a lot of energy in service to the goals of the team. Covert, high-stakes competition for perks within the organization (like promotions) can leave blood on the tracks. Don't deny the combative aspect of your natures. Really, there's no use in trying—they're there for both of you. Get them out in the open and put them in service to your outfit.

This can work in a marriage, too. Banter. Clever repartee. Open competition. Play fighting. Real fighting. Fair fighting. The thrill of victory, the agony of defeat. Many marriages continue from "I do" unto death with this constant spirit of battle as the glue that holds the couple together. Blues and Golds have a hard time understanding it, but it's none of their business anyway. Now, if you are an Orange/Blue and your partner is a Green/Gold, the spirit of the battle can easily turn sour since it may really be a battle between your second Colors, Blue and Gold. They don't know how to fight for the fun of it. They actually think that winning and losing may have eternal consequences. Fortunately for the true Orange–Green relationship, time is fleeting. Nothing lasts long. Round Seven. When you hear the bell, come out fighting. And don't forget to check out the gorgeous girl carrying the round-number card. Ah, Orange.

GREEN IN RELATIONSHIPS

Greens, I would like to invite you to turn your cool, appraising eye on relationships. Though I know that you tend to be very sufficient unto yourself, even the Greenest of us seeks companionship: perhaps wishing to raise children, perhaps hoping to find someone to share diverse or specialized interests, someone to share a physical relationship, and—above all, perhaps—someone to appreciate the intelligence and insight that you possess in abundance. Naturally, in addition, there are the inevitable and unavoidable relationships involved in work and professional activities.

Most Greens report that they have felt pressure in their lives to be more social, to be part of the group, the work team, or the family. Your need for independence in thinking and analyzing contributes to an impression of cool distance. Your needs for space, solitude, and time for processing add to people's misunderstanding. Your high demand for personal integrity has probably made it difficult for you to conform to the terms of belonging of the groups with which you've been involved. The subtlety and complexity of your thoughts get thrown into disarray when you try to fit in with irrationality, rigidity, or excess emotion. The gears don't mesh.

Greens have told me how wonderful it is to find someone who is really interested in their thoughts, really appreciative of their special knowledge and understandings, someone who really admires their wit and intelligence. "Whew!" they say; "what a relief not to be completely alone." Of course, in the next breath they express their gratitude for the space and solitude they still have. Or else they share their frustration with the loss of these precious commodities if they've had to give them up to make a relationship work.

Above all, they report what a joy it is to be appreciated for their unique contributions to the unfolding of the group, whether it is the academic discipline, the work group, the family, or the marriage. Greens often have deep fear of being perceived as uncaring and isolated. Your caution about communicating your deepest thoughts and feelings, your dedication to the integrity of your values and style, may have given the impression that you don't care to belong. At the same time, your ability to analyze and solve serious problems confronting the group demonstrates your contribution and the real value of your participation. Your commitment of time, effort, money, and thought to your spouse demonstrates your love. You make a contribution on your own terms. Your sexuality is not necessarily tied together with deep intimacy and personal affection. You show love in your own way. You always have. If only these things were recognized, the three little words wouldn't be necessary.

All of these challenges may be unfamiliar to you if you've been raised with people who have valued you as you are. In that fortunate case, you will know your own worth. You will approach relationships with a confidence born of that knowledge. The majority of your Green brethren will envy you your good luck as they deal with relationships filled with misunderstanding. If you know or work with other Greens, you will see all sorts of variations on these themes.

Green and Green

Ah, here comes someone with a mind! Great. Let's learn together. When Greens get together, there will either be an appreciative and understanding silence, or there will be a very interesting conversation.

If they have interests in common, there will be much to talk about in that field. If each person's premises and conclusions agree with those of the other, the conversation will move harmoniously and enjoyably through the information. There may be some competition about who knows best, but with common premises it should work itself out nicely. If the premises and conclusions are different, there will be a lively dispute, perhaps even a battle. Depending upon how much Orange the Green people share, this battle can be fun and exciting—or it can become bitter and divisive. You will have to be convinced before you will change your conclusions, and so will your partner or colleague. Or you may have to agree to disagree. This process can range from matters of child-rearing to marital behavior or serious professional disputation. Your tolerant attitude will usually come to your aid in dealing with differences, but the differences will not simply go away on their own.

In all your relationships, much depends upon your sense of safety with regard to the chance of looking foolish. As I've said before, humiliation is usually about the worst possible relationship experience for Greens. Discovering that you have been dead wrong, publicly, about something important; blundering into a position of illogic; being laughed at for your errors—these are deeply painful moments for most Greens. Other Greens are very good at discovering and pointing out such goofs, and they may not be particularly gentle about doing so. Thus differences about facts or principles can take on a very high-stakes energy for you in your relationships with other Greens.

On the other hand, no one can understand what these situations are like as well as another Green, and if you meet in an attitude of love and respect, your lives can be deeply enriched. It means a lot to have shared the "Green experience" growing up . . . the solitude, the intellectual interests, the social awkwardness, the sexual curiosity, the pressure to conform . . . it can be a wonderful thing to meet someone who understands. As with all Colors, the influence of your second Color will make a profound difference in these matters. Once you resolve these Green–Green issues, you will be left to enjoy or to struggle with the differences and commonalities that arise from your second Colors.

Green and Blue

When you cross paths with a Blue, you may find them to be rather mysterious . . . illogical, emotional, intuitive, tangled up in half a dozen confused relationships, enmeshed with their families, boundaryless, interested in all sorts of nonrational philosophies and experiences . . . just what the heck is going on with them?

It may be good news or bad news that they seem to be very interested in you! They care what you think and seem to have affection for you even before they know you very well. Instead of arguing with you when you have a difference, at least at first they try to understand. They may even express agreement, changing their position to make it harmonious with yours. You may not trust this kind of flexibility until you "get it" that what they care about is not the intellectual content so much as harmony in the relationship. For Blue, peace is often more important than intellectual integrity. They are willing to be wrong if it serves to smooth relations. Your life, on the other hand, is probably filled with situations in which you have chosen to be right instead of superficially happy.

Even more puzzling and sometimes annoying is the Blue's emotionalism. They seem to switch in a matter of moments from despair to joy and back again. Then they may become depressed for days over nothing. Or else they may become irrationally delighted or enthusiastic for weeks about some simple fact or event in the world, or—worse yet—become irrationally enthusiastic over something very suspicious or even obviously wrong.

Emotions often overrule facts, and the Blue may seem to be practically incapable of getting the facts straight. Sometimes you just can't reason with them. Sex is one and the same as emotion and communication to the Blue. There's no setting aside the emotional issues for a moment of physical enjoyment. There's no simple "setting the facts in order" so that intimacy can occur. Blues just don't divide life up into different areas. It's all one big homogeneous whole. When things are not in order, there is no sexuality.

Still and all, their intuitions often prove true. When they say, "I feel that thus and so may happen . . ." it fairly often does. They read other people well and know what it takes to please or displease others. They are socially pretty much at ease, meeting people where they are, shifting social Colors like a chameleon. Their kisses and hugs are heartfelt. Their love is genuine and it feels good to receive it . . . up to a point. They see your deep concerns and share them with easy passion. They even have words for all those subtle or even powerful emotions that sometimes seem to flood you beyond your control. They can actually help when the emotions boil over in you, as they occasionally do.

In work, Blues benefit from your quick intellect, and especially your ability to set boundaries. They really appreciate your help in sorting out the world, which to them is just one big mass of relationships. They also appreciate it when you express some vulnerability and uncertainty. They don't enjoy rubbing your face in it the way some others do, but seek out the best in you and try to help you get through the situation with as little pain as possible.

Then all of a sudden, they blow up in a white-hot anger like you've never seen before. They go for the knock out in the tirade that follows. They may accuse you of all those things you've heard before—of being uncaring and cold, of not sharing your feelings or not having any, and so on. They have been setting aside their own interests in service to you and feel that you haven't appreciated it, or in some other way they are feeling that a deep injustice is taking place. As a spouse, they may feel that you are not available to the children. As a coworker, they may feel that you are not sensitive to the needs of others. The surprising thing is the force of their rage. It's as strong as their love and passion. This is the biggest challenge of being with Blues.

Green and Gold

At last, here is a detail person. The Gold is someone who will cross the t's and dot the i's while you take care of the sophisticated data manipulation, solve the complex problems, and come up with the big ideas. The Gold can follow directions explicitly, even when they don't understand the underlying logic of the plan. They take work seriously and want it done right. They are never dreamy or emotionally volatile, and they don't play around on the job.

They value the impression they make on you and others. They put things in their proper places and find a time and a place for everything. They are a great help in keeping you in touch with the practical realities of daily life and the expectations of others as you pursue your inward agendas.

The Gold brings you a reality check, keeps a tidy house, keeps your calendar current and your important papers in some kind of order. They respect your work space and will tidy it if you wish, but they will also respect your boundaries as long as you don't impose your mess on them, which is more than they can stand. Here is someone who can finally keep order around you. If they are Gold/Blue, they will guide you through the complexities of the irrational world of emotions. If they are Gold/Green, they will join you in your seriousness and your commitment to productivity. If they are Gold/Orange, they will be a driving force moving you forward in an organized and energetic way.

Your Gold partner or coworker will be focused on concrete realities. They are not introspective; nor are they especially analytical. If anything, they will accuse you of thinking too much instead of acting, going off on tangents instead of carrying out practical tasks. They will appreciate your skill at problem solving more than the complex reasoning behind it. When it comes to expressions of love or appreciation, they will enjoy unwrapping presents and opening birthday cards. Like you, they value concrete expressions of love more than emotional words and sentiments. At work, they will appreciate public recognition and rewards more than any other Color. At home, they will value traditional holiday celebrations, family traditions, and a rewarding sexuality. If you value your relationship with a Gold, remember your anniversary! For solid, serious commitment, good order, and a meaningful place in the community, Gold will be your best bet.

Green and Orange

Hurrah for a fellow rebel! When it comes to poking holes in pompous, puffed-up authority figures, the Orange is for you. Some Oranges carry out their independent lifestyle quietly with occasional bursts of energy and excitement. Most of them wear their energy on their sleeve every day. Together, Green and Orange are a danger to everything conceited and tyrannical.

On the other hand, if you value your position, power, and authority, you may want to avoid the maverick Orange. At work, they will likely resist your attempts at micromanagement, preferring to receive clear objectives and timelines and to be left to their own devices in getting the job done—which they will do. Fortunately, this is most often Green's preferred style of management anyway, and when Oranges are on your side, they can't be beat for energetic action.

At home, their lives are lived for the joy of novelty, sensation, laughter, and impulsiveness. Your Orange spouse may not be too cautious about stepping on your toes or pointing out those embarrassing errors that we talked about above. If life is a game, then catching a smart person like you in an error is a definite win, even when they love you dearly. Still, they appreciate new things, and that includes new ideas, at least as long as they lead to action and the talk doesn't go on too long. Their enjoyment of sex usually includes a delight in novelty and adventure that you will probably find amusing and enjoyable. You'll rarely find an Orange sticking up for traditional ideas and values when new ones are being discovered or tested. Like you, the Orange is not caught up in the past, but looks at each day and each situation afresh.

You will share a love for clever and successful dealings in business, deal making, and professional matters. Oranges enter into these activities with the enthusiasm of an athlete and with a highly competitive zeal. You come to them with a serious, analytical shrewdness, but also with a great desire to win. The Orange will be more impulsive than you are, more willing to take risks for the thrill of it, but they want to win and there is a natural alliance between their competitive skill and your clever intelligence.

Orange is very social—not in the intimate and sensitive way Blues are, but with a gregarious, energetic, physical enthusiasm that can be very infectious. They may like team play while you may prefer more solitary sports or the rich intellectual tradition of baseball, for example. Orange loves an open competitive challenge, while you prefer to work at your own pace and reveal the power you have achieved in your own way and your own time, if you ever reveal it at all. You both love power in your different ways, and this can lead you to compete with each other for it unless you choose to join forces.

In your arguments, you will accuse the Orange of having a "ready, fire, aim!" mentality, of thoughtlessness and inconsistency. The Orange will counter that you think too much and are too serious for your own or their good. Both of you are more motivated by personal drives than by community interest. Your common tendency toward self-centeredness may make sharing and cooperation difficult at times, but the fact that you have it in common definitely helps. Chances are you will develop somewhat independent lives over time if you become partners. But however you choose to live, together you are the salt of the earth. Each of you brings a special savor that keeps the world from ever becoming dull and stuck in its ways.

Notice that there are six pairs of different Colors. There are ten pairs if you count the four same-Color combinations: Blue and

Blue, Green and Green, et cetera. There are twenty-four different orders that the four Colors can take in a Colors profile. In addition, if you look closely at the quiz, you'll notice that each Color's influence can be weak or strong as represented by the numerical score. Put all these differences together and the Color numbers have many thousands of different combinations of strengths. Ten pairs, twenty-four different profiles, thousands of patterns of relative strength . . . Colors does not reduce us to four simple types; far from it! Like the four cardinal points of the compass, there are infinite directions in between. But knowing North, East, South, and West is mighty helpful in finding our way.

CHAPTER 9

When the Colors Blend

Look at your first *two* Colors. There are six possible pairs. The effects of the second and even the third and fourth Colors can be very important. They give unique texture to every individual profile. It is very interesting to look at some of these subtleties, but it's also possible to get lost in a hurry if we try to go too deep. So let's take a look at the six pairs, which I have dubbed Sunburst, Mystic, Diamond, Firecracker, Torchbearer, and Homebuilder.

WHEN BLUE AND ORANGE BLEND—"SUNBURST"

Sunburst loves the bright, active, passionate life. You'll find him or her to be right-brained all the way, full of physical energy and lots of strong feelings that come bubbling out at all the right times—and also the wrong ones. Work is a very personal adventure, but highly engaged with other people. Love is emotional and creative, full of fantasy, fiery feelings, and experimentation. Sun burst demands the freedom to explore in a world of love and passion, while paying close attention to precious personal emotions, values, and possibilities. Physical energy is strong. The heart is lively. Moving, going, and doing combine with sensitivity.

Love is a passion. But so is everything else. Idealism is a big part of the passion. So is sexuality in a love affair or a marriage. Enthusiasm follows enthusiasm, with occasional bouts of exhausted depression. Negative feelings can be as strong as positive ones. Passionate anger can follow passionate affection. The anger can be a flash and gone, or sometimes it can be a lifelong preoccupation. Creativity is a very high value, and freedom an even higher one. Disorder and confusion may reign in practical matters. These are not Sunburst's concerns. Structure will need to come from outside, from other people or from social situations. The Blue/Orange Sunburst brings the energy; somebody else had better have the organizational chart.

Inner conflicts tend to occur between Sunbursts' powerful impulses to action and their concern for other people. Sometimes they simply must follow an impulse, even if it will cause pain to someone. Blue guilt will follow. Sometimes they suppress the impulse in service to someone else, and then find themselves feeling resentful and controlled. High energy and strong feelings are a double-edged sword for the Sunburst.

WHEN BLUE AND GREEN BLEND—"MYSTIC"

Here we go into a world of deep inner experience. The Mystic lives in a world in which deep thought interacts with profound feelings. Sacred texts, wise sayings, philosophical understandings—all are part of daily life. Dreams are important. They are thought over, talked over, perhaps interpreted according to some method or practice. Material things are seen in the light of their deeper meanings. Precious objects may be kept nearby, and may be assigned special value and power. The meanings of those objects are either deeply personal or seen as sacred to the collective. Matters of personal identity and spiritual influence are given close attention.

Lovemaking is a mystery, a spiritual journey, a way to be in contact with sacred energies or objects. Emotions are personal, to be shared with care and gentle respect. Gift giving takes on a deeply personal, often spiritual significance. Organized religious structures may be avoided or downplayed. The Mystic makes an independent spiritual journey. Certain places are filled with meaning. Visiting them and caring for them often has a ritual quality. Other cultures and ancient ways hold fascination.

The Mystic is very sensitive to shocks, both physical and emotional. The surface calm overlies reactive passions that run deep and strong below, and a delicate balance must be maintained. Small shocks can seem powerful jolts to the Mystic sensitivity. These are not people cut out for the rough-and-tumble of the marketplace. In all likelihood, they will strive to make for themselves a quiet space where inner exploration can go on with serene intensity.

Here, problems can occur around inwardness and passivity. It may be hard to act. Indecision and fear of others' reactions combine to suppress spontaneity. In addition, the sentimental Blue feelings argue with the Green rationality—and once again, action is postponed. There will be a tendency toward withdrawal as a preferred life strategy. This may or may not work out for the best.

WHEN GREEN AND GOLD BLEND—"DIAMOND"

Diamonds know the value of things and love quality. Pride and humiliation are the two ends of their measuring stick. Beauty, order, refined skill, special knowledge, careful appearances, and recognition—these are the hallmarks of success. Diamonds value physical attractiveness, careful hygiene, quality gifts given and received, good clothes, a well-cared-for home . . . class all the way. Responsibility, duty, and service are highly valued, and power is sought carefully and quietly. Diamonds appreciate being able to lead from behind. They wish to maintain a low profile while exercising an effective guiding hand.

Diamonds have a calm and deliberate demeanor. They express little emotion. Gushy sentiments seem shallow and gauche to them. They do not wish to be fawned over and have a hard time giving praise. But well-deserved recognition is not sentimental, and Diamonds wish to be recognized for the true value of their actions and way of life. In work, they feel that their rewards are justly earned, and they recognize the same worth in others. In love, duty and mutual respect are very important—but agreements carefully arrived at may allow for open marriage or other forms of independence. Family loyalty, diligent work, honorable service, a no-nonsense commitment to a community or a relationship . . . these are the real evidence of love to Diamonds. Love means doing and giving, not fine phrases or emotionalism. Careful analysis, correct and thoughtful action, tough but clear business dealings, respectful giving are the shining facets of the Diamond.

The conflict between the demand for action and the wish for "a little more information first" can keep the Diamond in a quandary. Impulses of social responsibility and goal-orientation are strong in the Gold side, while a desire for seclusion and autonomy arises from the Green. Sometimes a pattern of self-doubt results from this combination. There is also a tendency toward elitism stemming from the high standards and careful style of the Diamond. This can sometimes lead to resentment or even rebellion among associates.

WHEN ORANGE AND GREEN BLEND—"FIRECRACKER"

Hide your conceits; here come the devastating wits, the great stand-up comics, the masters of satire and irony. For a seminar leader, Firecrackers are the dreaded "trainer killers." They are independent, excitable, and have a very low tolerance for stuffed shirts. They love to poke fun at people who put on airs, people who are condescending to others. Firecrackers are not sentimental, and they're not impressed. The Orange side brings physical energy and social aggressiveness. The Green side brings sharp insights and clever language. Both Colors bring the demand for independence. All traditional ways are in danger!

Firecrackers think for themselves. They can be quite cantankerous and eccentric at times. They love clever ideas and ingenious things. Forever skeptical of others, they often fall in love with their own ingenious ideas. Firecrackers are not moved by a lot of talk about feelings and emotions. Their lovemaking is vigorous and creative, even eccentric. Both Green and Orange contribute to the pattern of deep feelings not talked about, even with closest friends and spouses. Romance is foreign to them. Anything mushy or touchy-feely is like fingernails scraping on a blackboard to Firecrackers.

In work, they will be masters of their specialty. In love, they will be autonomous and independent. You will rarely put anything over on them—though they may . . . on you.

When they reinforce each other, Orange and Green temperaments bring out a very sharp-tongued and sometimes tactless social style. Inwardly, the physical impulses and sensation-seeking of the Orange argue with the cool logic of the Green. Firecrackers often find themselves cleverly talking their way out of trouble once they've gotten there by following impulses.

WHEN ORANGE AND GOLD BLEND—"TORCHBEARER"

"In the beginning was the deed" would be a good motto for Torchbearers. They're full of drive, energy, and social responsibility. They carry the load and whistle while they work. They love tough tasks and laughter. They love accomplishment more than anything. They like to do things—fun things, productive things, team things. And they like to run things, they like to be in charge, and they usually run things very well. Just about every Torchbearer whom I've met has been a manager of some sort. Goals, purposes, timelines, schedules top their lists. And they do make lists, at least in their minds. A spirit of competition adds to the fun, along with a focus on concrete realities. Torchbearers are all action. Meditation is not on the agenda. They have a little difficulty relating to sensitive philosophy and mad emotionalism.

Torchbearer lovemaking is vigorous but it must fit into the schedule. It may or may not be a priority. While Torchbearers are very practical and energetic, they may not be highly emotional. Still, they value family and relationships highly. Gregarious and socially responsible, they sell the most tickets to the upcoming benefit concert, and they probably booked the orchestra and the hall and handled the publicity as well. Any organization is lucky to have them. If you're not looking for too much sentiment, a Torchbearer will make a loyal and fun life partner.

Speed seems to be the essence of the Gold/Orange Torchbearer. This combination can result in a highly aggressive personality, for better or for worse. Once again, we see the argument between the Orange impulses and, in this case, the orderly, goal-directed motives of the Gold. The Torchbearers I have known have reported the strongest internal conflicts of any of the combinations. Given the high energy and action orientation of both Colors, this shouldn't come as a surprise.

WHEN BLUE AND GOLD BLEND—"HOMEBUILDER"

Homebuilders are serious, down to earth, and tenderhearted. They love to care for places, people, children, animals, gardens, communities . . . in short, the world. Love is both emotional and responsible for Homebuilders. Lovemaking is a warm, affectionate, and natural act with deep roots in the home, in the meaningful relationship, and in the making of children. Commitment runs deep. It is expected in return . . . not a selfish possessive commitment, but a commitment to the things that matter and to practical efforts on behalf of those things.

Homebuilders are grounded in a deep feeling for the practical and meaningful things of the world, of nature, of home, and of the human community. Work is a part of this grounded commitment. Romantic love and deep personal loyalty are the foundation of sexuality for Homebuilder. Many hold to the view that sex is really for procreation—and even when it isn't, it should be treated with that same reverence. They could be called "Schoolteachers," since elementary schools, kindergartens, and preschools are staffed in large part by this combination of Blue and Gold. But beyond the schools, wherever service is the order of the day, there you will find Homebuilders in great numbers. They are playful and serious in their natural and proper seasons. I look for Homebuilders—solid, endlessly helpful—wherever I go. I know that they will help and guide me through whatever situation I find myself in.

The inner life of Homebuilders is a conversation between various sensitivities and sympathies on the one hand, and practical realities on the other. Both impulses tend to work for the good of those around them, which makes this combination so helpful in the community. Still, it's not always easy to resolve the tension between duty and compassion. A quiet sadness often results. Homebuilders often tell me that they wish they could change Colors. Personally, I'm very glad they're around.

CHAPTER 10

The Workplace

Leadership means managing people—one of the most difficult of all tasks. It means coordinating the actions of others in service to a common goal. It means establishing that goal and developing the consent of others to be governed by that goal. Each Color has its own way of carrying the burdens of leadership. Each has particular talents that lend themselves to good leadership, and each needs the support and, to some extent, the skills of the other Colors in order to be successful.

Working style, on the other hand, refers to the way people respond to the demands of work and the pressures of supervision. Each Color has its own motivations for performing and producing effectively. Each Color has its own satisfactions with regard to work, and what motivates one Color may be completely meaningless or even problematic to another.

Let's take a look at the various Colors' leadership and working styles.

GOLD LEADERSHIP STYLE

Golds are often in leadership positions, but they do not seek the limelight for its own sake. They are rarely moved by the desire for public visibility and fame. Golds lead because someone has to, because the work is important and must be done right, because they are personally committed and responsible, and because they value the status, the recognition, and the rewards. They accept positions of authority as the natural and inevitable result of their effort and dedication.

Hard work is the key to Golds' leadership style. They work hard themselves, and they expect others to do the same. Golds "do it the old-fashioned way: They earn it." It may be fun to find a dollar lying by the road, but it is deeply satisfying to earn one.

Golds have a sixth sense for what really needs to be done. In a business, in a family, in the community, Golds have an eye on the foundations, the necessities, the infrastructure, the moral and legal framework, and the bottom line. If something isn't getting done, they will do it or see that it gets done. They are usually decisive and sure of their ground.

Their standards are high. The ideals are clear and well defined. It takes a great deal of hard work to live up to them. In actual practice, though, those standards are hardly ever fully met. This means that Golds almost always see things falling short of their ideal. This is true even when things are going quite well. This sense of falling short drives them to expect more of themselves and of the people around them.

Golds are dedicated to the institutions they serve. This dedication applies to the family, the school, the business or corporation, the military organization, the nation, the ideology, the tradition, the religion, the way of life.

Gold leaders are always painfully aware of the potential for slip-ups, confusion, chaos, and failure. Delegation is a gamble.

"If something can go wrong, it will," is a Gold motto. This leads them to strive at all times for stability and good order, for well-defined procedures that must be carefully followed, and for tough accountability and real consequences. It is always a temptation for Golds to micromanage, since the farther from them the work is done, the less likely it is that the work will meet the standard.

Tradition is a primary value for Golds. The ways of the past are proven ways. Even if they may not be the most efficient and up-to-date, traditional ways have stood the test of time. Clever ideas and a fascination with the new for its own sake are frivolous. Once again, frivolous things threaten the foundations of order.

Organization is essential. Well-defined missions set the course. Plans implement it. Roles with defined responsibilities bring order out of the chaos of individual ideas, talents, and energy. Procedures coordinate the roles. Job descriptions and task analysis connect people to what must be done. Only in this way do day-to-day, moment-to-moment activities have their place in the grand scheme of things. Order out of chaos.

There must be accountability throughout the organization and conformity to the norms and policies. This means hierarchy, levels of responsibility, levels of authority. Managers must manage. Standards must be set and enforced. Subordinates must measure up. Golds are not shy about letting go someone who is not contributing. Sentiment has its place, but not at the expense of the organization. There is a sternness about a strong Gold. Expectations are high, and they are serious. This seriousness cuts both ways, and Golds feel the sting of their own failures most of all.

In negotiations, Golds strike a hard bargain. Contracts are at the core of working relationships. Tough bargaining means clear, enforceable contracts with the best possible terms. Golds know value. They believe in fairness, but they seek and respect competitive advantage as well. They are not sentimental about business relationships, though they do place a high value on loyalty and trust, on win–win solutions and cooperation wherever possible. Negotiation tends to be firm but fair.

Thoroughness, good use of time and energy, efficiency, punctuality—all are high values for Golds. Golds hate to be late. They are irritated when others are late. They make lists. Sometimes they make lists of lists. They often report that the next day is carefully planned before they go to sleep at night, the next week is pretty well thought out, and both fit into the plan for the month and the year.

Golds have a special relationship with money. To them, money is valuable in and of itself, and they love to see it accumulate. Spending is enjoyable when done with care and attention to value, but seeing the bank account grow, the net worth increase, the jars of jams and jellies row upon row in the larder . . . this is real satisfaction, safety, relief.

The outward and visible signs of success mean much to Golds. Money serves as one measure of that success, and Golds expect their pay to be commensurate with their efforts and their position. They don't like to see money lying idle. It should be working and earning just like people.

Every bit as important as money, however, is public recognition. Honors, testimonials, certificates of appreciation, promotions based on merit, Citizen of the Year—these can mean more than money for the Gold. So often it seems that no one knows how hard they really have worked, how much they have contributed. Spontaneous recognition of their achievement brings tears of gratitude and profound joy.

GOLD WORKING STYLE

Golds take work very seriously. They often report that a job well done is their highest joy. They want to contribute, to be successful and productive, and they respond well to recognition, rewards, and incentives.

Golds fill the ranks of management at every level. They make good administrators and respond well to shouldering important responsibilities. Public administration is a popular field with Golds, and they represent their institutions with dedication.

In the professions, Golds are orderly and productive. In medicine, they gravitate toward clearly defined specialties and often find their way to medical administration. In law, they lean toward the corporate and financial side, administrative law, prosecutorial positions, and the bench. Law enforcement is another popular occupation for Golds.

Auditing, accounting, home economics, and fiscal responsibilities are a natural fit for orderly Golds. They are attracted to the military, where they make decisive leaders and responsible soldiers.

Along with the Blues, Golds swell the ranks of public education and institutional health and social services. They make solid, responsible teachers and education administrators. In hospitals and clinics, they are nurses, technicians, orderlies, and clerical staff. They make fine librarians, curators, and archivists. They also provide support services throughout both public and private institutions, handling clerical and custodial jobs efficiently.

Their teaching style emphasizes community, tradition, and values. They establish clear expectations, and their discipline is firm and fair. The expectations come from traditional standards . . . the three r's and plenty of drill and practice.

In an office or factory, Golds prefer useful tasks, and they handle detail well. They mistrust abstractions, preferring to deal with the concrete. They like clear structure, firm expectations and timelines, and well-defined responsibilities, a clear notion of right and wrong. They need to know that they are on track, and they look to people in authority to tell them. They are punctual, arriving on time and leaving on time.

Golds make good salespeople. They present a good appearance, and they have the ability to order and organize the work of selling so that contacts are made and followed up, details are handled, time is well utilized and closing is solid. Selling requires hard work, persistence, and organization, and Golds often take to it well.

Golds also do well in merchandising. Their strong sense of value and their easy way with order and bookkeeping make them good buyers and managers throughout the retail and wholesale worlds. Golds love quality things, and they love a good appearance. Hairdressing, cosmetology, and retail apparel sales are favorite fields for them.

Golds make good employees. If they have a clear idea of what is expected of them and if the rewards are sufficient for their needs, they will be hardworking and productive.

BLUE LEADERSHIP STYLE

For Blues, the central driving force in leadership style is commitment to the people involved and to a strong sense of community. Blue leaders want to nurture people, to see the best come out in each member of the group. They are oriented to individual strengths, to relationships, and to participation.

Indeed, participation is a key value. Blues are reluctant to exercise arbitrary authority. Instead, they seek consensus based on communication and involvement. They are willing to be patient. They will sacrifice a certain amount of well-regulated efficiency in favor of maintaining harmony in relationships. The whole idea of team or community is very important to Blues.

These personal and community values lead Blues toward a democratic management style. They value input and pay serious attention to the points of view of employees or coworkers, whom they tend to think of as fellow participants in a joint venture. Blues give abundantly of appreciation and support. They want to be loved, and they want to manage with love.

Blues like flexible and creative solutions that arise from the people involved. They favor flexible procedures and put a high value on day-to-day learning and adaptation.

It is usually uncomfortable for a Blue to adopt an attitude of authority. Laying down the law can be very difficult. Blues are fundamentally egalitarian in their outlook, and the idea of one person lording it over another pushes a hot button of indignation or shame.

Tough negotiations can be a real challenge for Blues. Their desire for consensus and win–win solutions can undermine their ability to strike a hard bargain. Their aversion to people's dissatisfaction and conflict can make closing a deal a real nightmare for them.

Closing a sale or a deal is usually a bumpy process under the best of circumstances. Often, no one is completely satisfied. Empathetic Blues go to the utmost to keep everyone happy. They may well feel buyer's remorse in advance for all sides. On the other hand, this careful, empathetic approach and the consuming desire to please can lead to great teamwork, to very solid and satisfactory outcomes, and to considerable customer loyalty.

Having to fire someone, to let someone go, is nearly always traumatic for the Blue manager. It is one of those "little deaths" that Blues try to avoid at all costs. As leaders or managers, Blues will usually bend over backward to avoid having to do so. It is a common experience for Blue managers to lie awake nights, losing sleep over the incompetence or disruptiveness of an employee, while postponing the inevitable confrontation.

That powerful Blue anger, that righteous wrath that can wither flowers, will sometimes come out in crisis situations. There may be a long period of avoiding conflict and confrontation. But at some point, there will be enough wrongs or a last straw, and a real outburst is due. When the outburst comes, it can be frighteningly powerful and may lead to long-term regrets and recriminations.

In addition, when Blues lose confidence in themselves, when they feel ashamed and defeated, or when they feel that they have done harm, their depression can be deep and infectious. A kind of paralysis can set in, and it will last until the cloud lifts, usually through making amends, receiving emotional support, finding a sense of forgiveness, and arriving at a new inspiration. It is tough for Blues to move on from disaster. Loss of trust in others is very hard to repair.

In addition to all these people-centered aspects, there is a special visionary quality to the Blue leadership style. Blues are holistic thinkers. They see a big picture and they are inspired by what they see. They often have the ability to inspire others with the vision.

Such vision and emotion result in an enthusiasm that can be an infectious motivator. Suddenly, going to the moon sounds like a really beautiful idea, or gathering the family for a wonderful get-together in a new setting, or moving the company into fascinating, uncharted seas.

Blues are usually good communicators. They convey not only the idea, but also the feeling behind the idea. They are catalysts, and can rally the troops to new heights of endeavor, holding out an exciting vision for all to see, expressing deep faith in the abilities of the people around them.

Strong Blues are deeply intuitive. They look inside and get readings on things that the other Colors often miss. When a Blue says, “I've got a feeling about this,” it's usually a good idea to listen carefully. Their hunches sometimes border on ESP, if not actually going over the line into that strange domain.

Blues want to educate, to lead people toward meaningful things. They are drawn to the arts and to the spiritual dimension of life. They will move companies toward community involvement, toward doing well by doing good, investing for the long term in customer loyalty and social participation, caring for the environment even at some cost to the bottom line.

Cooperation, inspiration, personal growth, community development, investment for the good of all . . . these are watchwords for the Blue leader.

BLUE WORKING STYLE

As employees or group members, Blues wish for an open social atmosphere. They naturally form relationships with coworkers, customers, and employers, and they need the freedom and permission to care for these relationships. When the demands of the work, strict supervision, or organizational culture prohibit such relationships, Blues will suffer.

They value honesty, but not brutal honesty. To Blues, honesty equates to fair dealing and a lack of manipulation. Blues will tell little white lies, and even some pretty big ones, to avoid inflicting emotional pain, or to protect themselves from pain. Still, they are very sensitive to and suspicious of confidence games and motivational strategies. Blues give their best when they feel that they are trusted and can trust in return.

Emotional support is a key factor for Blues. They will give it, and they need to receive it. When Blues are left without feedback, they assume the worst about themselves. This leads them to spiral down into anxiety, self-doubt, and depression. Good, clean information about performance delivered in a caring and supportive manner does the trick.

Blues often value another person's affection more than his or her praise or admiration. "I'm glad you're here. I sure enjoy working with you. You're a real asset to the team"—all are high praise to a Blue.

Blues thrive in a positive, creative, service-oriented environment. They are troubled by intense competition. Conflict is painful. Heavy production orientation and mechanization may block relationships. Manipulative selling strategies and sharp business practices offend them and make them anxious. Blues fear meeting dissatisfied customers in the future and facing the shame of not having served them well.

They make good doctors, nurses, medical technicians, and hospital workers based on their excellent bedside manner. This is based more on their love of people than on easy technical mastery. The emotional suffering of patients can be hard for Blues. Harder still can be the apparent callousness of some medical professionals about a patient's pain.

Blues' love of people in general attracts them to the helping professions. They do well as clergy and in service positions related to church or charitable organizations. They do well in the service sector generally. They make great receptionists and public relations people. They present their best face to the community and represent the business or institution in a positive manner. In the office, they look to the needs of the staff as well as the customer.

Along with Golds, Blues tend to dominate the education, counseling, and social-service professions. As teachers, they are attracted to the early grades by their love of children. They put participation at the top of the priority list and work to develop student self-esteem, bringing out the best in each student's unique makeup. Discipline is usually personal, flexible, and inclusive, and they rely for motivation on inspiration and appreciation more than duty and consequences.

Blues are often artistic or musical with good speaking and writing skills. They are attracted to the arts and humanities and make good media people, creative marketers, actors, and entertainers. The opportunity to express feelings in creative ways is a real joy to Blues. The magic and mystery of the arts spread over into the realm of the spiritual, which is usually a Blue's highest aspiration.

ORANGE LEADERSHIP STYLE

Orange leaders are focused on action. When they are bright and talented, when they have the resources, when they have the bit in their teeth, the sky's the limit. Action is at the center. Institutional structures and procedures are never an end in themselves. Everything else exists to make action possible. Everything that blocks or frustrates action must be set aside.

Deeply bound up with action is skill. Skill in action. "Show me the problem, give me the tools, and get out of the way!" "Call in the guys who know what they're doing, and turn them loose on the job!" "Get me the best!" Time present. Here and now. Let's get to work.

The tools must be in hand. The right tool for the job. If the right tool isn't handy, we'll invent it. Troubleshooting is our middle name. Getting the bugs out. Improvising. Making it work.

Oranges are blessed with an entrepreneurial spirit. They love to work for themselves, to be their own boss, set their own pace, and work to the best of their ability. In middle management they respond well to project assignments when they are given the latitude to get the job done in their own way.

Oranges lead by example, setting a standard of performance for others to follow. Coaching is a good metaphor for the Orange style. They learn by doing. They don't enjoy learning from manuals or from verbal instructions, and they teach as they learn, more by showing than by telling. Cheerleading, enthusiasm, and encouragement combine with strong expectations, pushing the coworker, the student, or the employee to perform.

Orange leaders can be quite brusque and authoritarian in their management style. They are impatient with opposition, and they expect their directions to be followed. They are usually going full throttle themselves, and slowness or resistance in others feels like a very bumpy road. Orange leaders often physically touch people, moving bodies around with a matter-of-fact and playful strength. "Stand here. Grab hold here. Lift and release. If they push hard, you push harder!"

This intrusive style is frequently tempered by an infectious sense of humor, a feeling of genuine physical camaraderie, and a natural ability to move on from difficult situations without much ado. Oranges are capable of holding grudges and of acting on them. Still, their general here-and-now orientation keeps them moving forward in a positive way most of the time.

Oranges are realists. Their goals are concrete, actual, material. Action is physical. There must be movement. Less talk, more do! Get the job done and move on to the next one. The abstract is of little interest to them. Opportunities. Results. Product. Dollars. Winning.

Did someone say winning? Oranges compete! Competition means everything, and competition is to win. Oranges often report that winning is better than sex, and they usually like sex a lot. The Orange leader is competing all the time, competing with past performance, with business or sports competitors, with others within the organization, with heroes and significant figures from the past, with deeply held personal goals.

Orange leaders use competition as a motivator. They enjoy

managing via competition, challenging employees and coworkers to outdo one another, and leaping right into the fray themselves. Oranges like to see their coworkers physically active and competitive off the job as well. They expect it.

This competitive, entrepreneurial spirit makes for master negotiators, deal makers, and deal closers. Oranges' good verbal skills combine with tactical cleverness and a deep understanding and enjoyment of the game. Someone else can watch out for the incidentals. Orange negotiators are thinking many moves ahead, and they have their eye on the prize.

Above all, Orange leaders welcome change. The old ways can be improved upon. The new is an adventure, a challenge, the very stuff of life. Oranges are flexible and confident. Fear is the enemy, a waste of time. Utter devastation and complete failure are just events along the way. People are tough. They're not made of porcelain and crystal. They fall down. They break. They mend. They get up. They go on. "How else have we ever gotten anywhere that was worth a damn, anyway?" says the Orange.

ORANGE WORKING STYLE

Oranges love to work. They are sometimes thought of as too carefree and playful to be good workers. As young people, they are often turned off to traditional kinds of work when it's boring and when bosses are too authoritarian. It's easy to thwart and block their potential with too much structure and suppression. When Oranges are doing what they love to do, they are the hardest workers of all the Colors.

As in their leadership style, the key factors for Orange are energy and skill and the freedom to use them. It is very common for an Orange to work at something from dawn until late at night. The clock has no meaning. Punishment and reward are forgotten. All that matters is the challenge of the task at hand. Productivity is sky-high when work is play.

Oranges turn tasks into creative play. They love to develop their skills and performance to the highest possible level. The quiet Orange craftsperson may linger endlessly over creative detail work. The highly physical and mobile Orange construction worker may strive to outdo the previous day's performance. They love economy, precision, and grace in movement, finding the most efficient and elegant way to get the job done.

Movement, variety, and immediacy bring out the best in Oranges. They thrive on crisis situations and love to think on their feet. Physical problem solving is a natural strength. Sensory and concrete, they are grounded in the realities of tools and materials.

At their most skilled, they make excellent surgeons and craftspeople of the highest order. They are attracted to engineering and technical fields where they may work with materials either on the most massive scale or on the most intricate and delicate.

Oranges are tool users. Show an Orange a backhoe, a bulldozer, a police car, an ambulance, or an airplane, and he or she will want to climb aboard, turn it on, and go. Give them a soldering iron, a metal lathe, a scroll saw, or a scalpel and they will want to put it to use immediately.

Oranges love to build things. I know an eighty-year-old Orange man who decided one day that he needed a twenty-four-foot-square, two-room cottage on a corner of his property. After eyeballing the site, the man excavated it with pick and shovel, built the forms, poured the foundation, framed the walls and roof, finished the exterior and interior in fine style, and was ready to move in in a couple of weeks, all without a single plan on paper!

Farming, ranching, forestry, fishing, hunting, guiding—Oranges naturally love the outdoors. They love the independence, self-reliance, and endurance that go along with working outside.

Oranges like people, and they work with people in a spirit of teamwork, competition, and camaraderie. Teaching, coaching, and youth work are often a good fit. Oranges love children. They frequently have a natural, unforced rapport and an easy authority with young people.

As teachers, the Oranges rely on an up-tempo style with lots of hands-on activity and group camaraderie. They tend to keep the structure pretty fluid, with lots of room for taking advantage of the unexpected. Learning is concrete, visible, and relevant. Discipline is usually built around a sense of team building, challenge, enthusiasm, and personal responsibility without strong traditional value judgments. The Orange teacher is sometimes prone to power struggles.

In business, selling is a strong point. Though Orange salespeople may need help around the detail work, they have an instinct for the bottom line. Their enthusiasm and love of the chase give them energy galore, and they capitalize on every opportunity to move the customer toward the close.

Law enforcement and public safety work appeals to the Orange sense of adventure. Technical specialties like nursing, dental hygiene and assisting, or respiratory therapy give Oranges the opportunity to be moving and doing with skill.

Oranges are not natural followers, and they thrive on the

opportunity to build all the skills necessary for an independent life. Their entrepreneurial tendencies can take them in any direction in which skill and self-reliance pay off. A few examples that I know of include an independent chef with his own small, quality catering business; a pushcart vendor in an open-air market; and the owner of a toy factory deep in the woods. For Oranges, the possibilities are endless.

Oranges also make great entertainers in all fields. Wherever they work, they bring fun, humor, witty conversation, and energy. A workplace without the Orange influence can be a pretty dull place.

GREEN LEADERSHIP STYLE

Greens bring intellect, ingenuity, pragmatism, and design to the leadership role. Working smart is what matters to Green . . . seeing the whole picture, understanding the details that make it up, relating the details to the whole, creating pathways and activities that move things forward, applying technology, solving problems, and adjusting goals in a realistic way.

The Green leader tries to take account of the whole complex field of factors and influences in a situation. This means thorough assessment, sufficient information, careful reasoning based on the information, planned action, attention to feedback, and adaptation to new information. Greens don't shoot first and ask questions later. They don't defend the old in the face of the new. They aren't moved by sentiment and enthusiasm. They want to follow the facts wherever they lead.

The big picture is apparent to Greens. The analytical Green mind synthesizes, drawing on a broad field. All the detailed care and deliberation must relate to the whole. Greens work conceptually, relating information to constructs and paradigms that make sense to them. These underlying ideas are often rooted in theories and philosophies that cross disciplines and go well beyond the task at hand.

Greens can explain what they are doing. They can explain what their organizations are doing. They can explain their expectations and instructions to their subordinates and coworkers. Often their understanding and explanations go well beyond the ability of others to understand. This can be a problem for the Green leader.

Greens have an uncanny ability to sort out complex situations and design systems to manage them. It is a real delight to watch this Green mind at work, weighing and measuring, categorizing and systematizing, anticipating and planning, creating tools and processes that meet many contingencies and challenges.

The big-picture view is the strategic view. Greens make strategy, and they make it for the long term. In addition to attending to the dynamics within their organization, family, or group, Greens take account of the larger movements around their organization and position things accordingly.

The Green leader uses schematic diagrams, illustrates concepts and processes, makes maps, develops grids and diagrams, and lays out pathways. Greens tend to be systemic thinkers, working from the whole to the part and back again. This analytical process is second nature to Greens. It's fun for them, the most fun there is.

Whenever relevant, science and technology are familiar necessities to Greens. They are proud of their skill and knowledge in complex technical fields, and they enjoy being the specialist in a field of laypeople. They keep themselves up to date on the latest developments and enjoy applying them in ingenious ways.

Certain things are to be avoided at all costs, most particularly any form of stupidity. Greens detest stupidity. Stupid things include redundancy, confusion, emotionalism, hidebound traditionalism, irrationality, and impulsiveness.

Redundancy is a particular bugaboo for Greens. It is practically impossible for Greens to repeat themselves. They just can't get the words out. "It's already been said, for heaven's sake. Weren't you listening? You already said that. Do you think I didn't understand?" Green readers will notice that this has been said in a previous chapter.

Green leaders expect people to pay attention, to be genuinely interested, and to get it the first time. Repetition is an insult to everyone's intelligence, and that's a very great sin. This expectation that people will pay attention and understand is a key to the Green's leadership style. Greens give the information and move on. Failure to act on the information is the listener's responsibility.

Individual autonomy and responsibility are also strong values for Green. They are very reluctant to exercise power over others. Stating the facts of the case should be sufficiently compelling. Intelligent minds should work together around the data and the plan. As independent individuals, we either cooperate or we go be independent somewhere else. Greens are not sentimental about these things. Firing someone seems almost overdramatic. A parting of ways should be obvious from the facts of the situation.

Greens love to teach. They want to contribute to growth and

competence in others and to enrich the volume of knowledge in an organization. They frequently lead by instructing, teaching principles and techniques that others are to apply. They like to bring in outside experts, good reading materials, interactive learning tools and training. Learning is a catalyst to Green, stimulating creative problem solving and ingenuity. Research is essential to organizational functioning.

The niceties of social interaction tend to escape Green leaders. They are not much interested in subtleties of feeling and relationship. In fact, they don't pay much attention to them. Their leadership style is rather dry, focused on the vision and on analysis of tasks and information. They are not overly given to praise and give little thought to emotional support. The facts speak for themselves. Good work is good work. Everyone knows it. Why all the fuss?

GREEN WORKING STYLE

Greens like to know why they're doing what they're doing. The rationale is everything. They need the freedom to arrive at their own conclusions, and to act on them. Greens think for themselves.

In the workplace or profession, Greens are motivated by curiosity. Their minds tend to probe deeply into things, pursuing underlying structure, process, and significance. They do their best work in this way. Given free rein, Greens develop understanding, and they can make a major contribution to any setting.

They love data and information of all kinds. They read. They compute. They analyze. They understand specs. They strategize.

They design. Then they move on. Routine follow-through is not their strong suit.

Greens love the abstract and the intellectual, in technology, in the arts and humanities, in scientific research, in systems design, in management, in education, in comic books, in video games, in science fiction. Greens learn and teach. They write and do research.

Their focus is on the information. They are skeptical and analytical. They don't settle for easy answers and they mistrust glibness, tradition, and sentiment. Greens pride themselves on not being gullible. They often possess a dry and trenchant wit and sometimes a scathing tongue. They do not suffer fools gladly, and they refuse to be fools themselves.

In the law, they love the intricacies of argument, the fine detail of precedent, ingenious case making, stratagems, telling facts, and the demonstration of compelling and powerful intelligence. In science and medicine, they are attracted to the cutting edge of research and theory, the subtleties of evidence, rigorous and relentless analysis, absolute expertise, the finely honed specialty.

Computers are a playland for Greens, requiring all their analytical skills, all their intelligence and ingenuity. Data analysis, engineering, and systems design often leave the other Colors behind, but here Greens can come into their own.

Greens are not highly social and gregarious by nature. They do best in fields that give them a little distance in relationships. Photography and journalism are two common examples.

In any work setting, Green workers need this sense of space. They are independent by nature, and they don't like to promote themselves. They do, however, want to be recognized and utilized for their intelligence, their competence, and their pragmatic vision. They find their way into management based on their expertise in the field, rather than on their natural people skills.

As teachers, they are brought to education by whatever subject area they are teaching; by the content more than by the students. They tend to be attracted to the higher grades where content is more sophisticated. They expect their students to be there out of interest in the information and to be self-motivated. For this reason, their disciplinary style tends to be very laissez-faire with strong reliance on natural consequences and learning through experience.

In the open market, Greens can sell very well in technical fields where information and expertise sell the product, but they are shy about cold calling and the other extrovert people skills that come into play in general sales. They are ingenious at creating marketing strategies, but would rather get the other Colors to make the calls.

This is a key factor in managing the Green worker to best advantage. They do best at the analytical, creative level—research, data management, analysis, design, teaching—and routine follow-through is often best left to others.

Green workers are unique, and usually very much in the minority. They can be quite touchy, withdrawn, even eccentric. But their special gifts are essential in any dynamic organization. They often need special care if their gifts are to flower.

The next page lists some suggestions about the particular fields of work that are often enjoyed by the different personality styles.

SAMPLE OCCUPATIONAL PREFERENCES BY COLOR

Gold

Administrators
Managers
Factory or site supervisors
Clerical supervisors
Surgeons
Lawyers
Dentists
Social-service workers
Police, detectives
Auditors, accountants
Retail and commission sales
Military
Nurses
Health technicians
Medical secretaries
Editors
Teachers
Librarians
Clergy
Home economists
Hairdressers
Cosmetologists

Blue

Clergy
Educators
Physicians
Nurses
Media specialists
Teachers
Education consultants
Librarians
Psychiatrists
Psychologists
Social workers
Marriage and family counselors
Rehabilitation workers
Child-care workers
Service-sector business
Writers
Artists
Editors
Musicians
Entertainers

Orange

Engineers	Heavy-equipment operators
Electrical technicians	Emergency technicians
Mechanics	Managers, administrators
Teachers	Entrepreneurs
Coaches	Commission sales
Farmers	Auditors
Dental assistants	Child-care workers
Dental hygienists	Receptionists
Storekeepers	Religious workers
Nurses	Musicians
Bookkeepers, accountants	Performing artists
Marketing personnel	Artisans
Police, detectives	

Green

Lawyers	Librarians
Researchers	Writers
Physical scientists	Artists
Social scientists	Entertainers
Doctors, surgeons, medical technicians	Photographers
Computer programmers	Marketing personnel
Systems analysts	Sales (technical)
Chemical engineers	Journalists
High school teachers	Managers, administrators
University teachers	Mortgage brokers
	Accountants

CHAPTER 11

Children

THE GOLD CHILD

Gold children need security based on an orderly life and on high standards of quality and effort. Concrete, practical realities are of the highest significance to them. The ground under their feet must feel secure. The lawn needs to be mowed. The roof mustn't leak. The baby needs changing. Meals should be on time.

From an early age, Gold children will try to correct anything that threatens the order around them. Parents can expect their Gold children to parent *them* if need be; to correct their language, to resist their impulsiveness or impracticality, to count their money, to judge their competence, their house, their cars, their success. There is often a comic seriousness to the righteous attitudes of the Gold child.

Security and order mean predictability to Gold children. Accustomed and proven ways are best. Novelty and new ideas are not to be trusted. New situations are very challenging, and they are met with ordering strategies from the past. Knowing what's worked before, who's in charge, and what the rules are brings safety.

Gold children appreciate routine, and they like to organize

things. They are very good at meeting the demands of everyday life in an orderly way. When routines are disrupted, they become confused and anxious. There may be clutter, but rarely is there mess. If there is mess, it is *their* mess and they know how it works. Certain things need to be done at certain times in certain ways, day by day.

Roles and defined relationships are important to Gold children. This is Uncle John. Uncle John does certain things and doesn't do others. Grandpa is Grandpa. Grandma is Grandma. Father is a certain way. Mother another. Older siblings have their roles. Younger siblings theirs. The cop on the beat has his or her job. Just as the firefighter, the teacher, the minister, and the doctor do. And I have my role, too. These things are fundamental. They are not to be tampered with.

Rules go right along with roles. There are certain ways to act and not to act. These rules come from proper authority. They are handed down from the past. Justice should be swift and sure when the rules are violated. Consequences should be fair, appropriate, and immediate. Injustice or chaotic justice is deeply upsetting and confusing. Somehow, order must be restored.

This emphasis on roles and rules goes along with a need and respect for authority. Gold children are obedient to legitimate authority, and they see most authority as legitimate. They have a strong sense of right and wrong based on the "shoulds" and "oughts" that come from tradition. They see nothing wrong with the stern and proper exercise of power in the name of order. In their turn, they expect their own authority—whether it comes from their birth order, their family role, or their social position—to be respected and obeyed.

Territory and ownership are strong values for Gold children. It is my toy box, in my room, in our house, in our town, in our state, in our country. Boundaries must be set and respected. Property is sacred. Ownership is a right. Stewardship is a responsibility.

Along with rules, roles, authority, territory, and ownership go appropriate rewards and deserved status. Gold children pay careful attention to who has earned what, and they expect just rewards for their efforts. They are strongly motivated by honors and recognition. They work hard and carry much responsibility, and it is only right that they should receive their due praise and be paid well.

Appearances are always important to Gold children. Quality work and an orderly workshop are essential. When company comes, appearances are to be preserved. If there must be mess, it should be tucked away to be cleaned up later. Roles and responsibilities in the family and community require that we present ourselves decently. Neatness of dress and appearance mean a great deal. How we are seen by others is a fundamental concern. Serious developmental education such as education about sex need to be handled in a calm manner that stresses natural order and safety.

Gold children pay attention to time. They are punctual and dependable and they get the job done. Work before play is an obvious necessity. In school, they expect an orderly and traditional classroom, practical and profitable, with concrete learning, fair rewards and punishments, and public recognition for a job well done. They contribute to the family and community. They do their duty. They preserve tradition and look out for the continuity of the past.

Gold children are no more angels than any other Color. They can be very stubborn and willful, especially in relationship to an emotional Blue, a playful Orange, or an abstract Green. In general, however, they tend to make less trouble than other children. This can be a burden for them, and sometimes the potential joy and adventure of childhood get lost in the search for security and accomplishment.

THE BLUE CHILD

Blue children are emotionally sensitive and reactive. Feelings are always near the surface. From the earliest times, Blue children cry and laugh easily. Unhappiness and discomfort are intense. Happiness and merriment are infectious. Life is an emotional roller coaster. Sleep may be restless and full of dreams. The Blue child responds to attention and can be very rewarding to the parent, deeply engaged and responsive from the beginning. The happy Blue child is helpful and supportive of others, a contributing member of the family.

When Blue children feel emotionally safe, they are very social, gregarious, and responsive to the people around them. They like to have lots of friends, and they look for intimacy in the family. They often act as a sort of emotional barometer of what's going on among the people around them.

This interpersonal sensitivity is keyed to the rises and falls of persons in the rough-and-tumble of daily life. Persons are precious to Blues. The social successes and failures, gains and losses, triumphs and humiliations of people have life-and-death importance for the Blue child. Unfairness and injustice are very significant. Social failure and rejection are crushing. Blue children root for the underdog.

This social sensitivity reaches below the surface of things.

When people around them are wearing masks, smoothing over their conflicts and difficulties, being sneaky and mean under a respectable facade, the intuitive Blue child senses these undercurrents and reacts to them. While the child may not be permitted to react openly, he or she will show distress in moodiness, sullenness, illness, misbehavior, and sometimes open rebellion. A good question to ask a child showing these behaviors is, "Is this a mad thing or a sad thing you're feeling?" It will usually be one or the other.

Attachment is a key to Blue children: attachment to objects, to people, to pets, to special places, to books or ideas. Loss is an especially important theme in their lives. Blue children mourn deeply, and they mourn a long time. This mourning may be about things that seem trivial to the other Colors—a toy, a doll, an article of clothing, a special activity with a special person. Major losses can be really debilitating for them.

Blue children are often highly imaginative, even dreamy. They love to pretend. Their inner life is usually full of imagery, and the images are full of emotional significance. They are often spontaneously artistic or musical, and their creations can have real insight and power from an early age. Their imagination can take them to the heights of joy and inspiration and to the depths of fear and despair. Dreams and nightmares are powerful. Blue children invest an almost magical significance in certain key symbols. They learn well from symbolic play—dolls, sandbox play, art, charades, music—Blue children will reveal their inner world in their play.

Blue children often need help with structure and motivation. Their dreaminess, imaginative fearfulness, and emotionality sometimes undermine their ability to act, to do rote learning, or to carry out repetitive tasks that need to be done. They don't respond easily to rigid structures. They move more naturally and easily with flexible routines. But they do not seek chaos, either. Emotional safety is the key, for themselves and for the people around them. If structure keeps people safe and happy, it is welcome. If it is punitive, arbitrary, and unjust, it is rejected.

As with all their emotions, anger is strong for Blue children. It can be quite startling when the sensitive, artistic, and nurturing Blue child suddenly lets loose with righteous wrath, indignation, or injured rage. This anger easily becomes sullen and brooding if it doesn't clear. It is part of the price of leading with the heart, making strong attachments, and valuing personal justice so highly.

Blue children need emotional nourishment and support. As with Blue adults, they feel hurt by criticism and assume the worst from silence. In the classroom, they do well when they are inspired, intrigued, allowed to dream and create in an open, interactive environment. While they need external help with boundaries, limits, and deadlines, they thrive on loving touch and encouraging words. While they want to express themselves and their creative imagination, Blue children will choose belonging and harmonious relationships over success.

Competition is not motivating to Blue children. It threatens the smooth emotional flow that they seek. Victory at too great a cost to someone else is uncomfortable to Blues.

Duty in the abstract doesn't carry much weight with them, either. It is the personal aspect of duty, the emotional responsibility to another, that will motivate them.

Serious developmental learning usually takes place through what is modeled by others. Blue children are particularly attuned to what is communicated between the lines. No matter what is being said, it's what people actually do and—above all—what people actually feel that Blue children respond to. If they see warm, loving touch and contact between parents and other adults, it's the most wonderful feeling in the world to them, and the best possible sex education and relationship education generally. All their lives, it will be the relationships among the people around them that give them their sense of safety or threat.

Blue children are not selfless and endlessly in service to others. They can be quite selfish. Often they avoid hurting others because that hurt may come back around on them in the future. Blues are not just altruistic. Their pain is powerful, and it is primarily their own pain they fear. But they feel pain when others feel pain, and that is a very powerful influence and restraint upon their behavior.

THE ORANGE CHILD

Orange children are physically active. They love challenges and they take risks, girls and boys equally. They need boundaries for safety, but within the boundaries they need room to move. Striking this balance between boundary making and freedom is the challenge in caring for Orange children.

Structure and routine are a real challenge for them. They are not naturally inclined toward order and boundaries. Safety is not of the highest concern. They love danger and have a high tolerance for pain. They are proud of their endurance and their toughness. A parent's worry and concern simply feel like fussiness and interference.

In fact, worry and concern are not a good approach to keeping Orange children safe. They need a more direct authority, even a physical authority, and it needs to be conveyed in a spirit of strength, respect, and camaraderie.

The Orange child responds well to a straight-from-the-shoulder, in-your-face kind of supervision. The caregiver's message needs to be, "You are strong. I love how strong you are. I am strong, too. We are both strong, and for your own safety I'm in charge of you!" Underlying this authority, there needs to be a real affection and respect for the Orange child's energy, skill, and creativity. To respond well, the child needs to respect the authority and to feel respected in return.

If a parent tries to plead with the Orange child, or to wheedle him or her into cooperating, the child loses respect and the authority is undermined. If the parent is a pushover, it will be more of the same. If the parent tries to simply dominate, however, exercising arbitrary authority based on the parental role, the Orange child is likely to rebel. What works is a relationship of strength between equals, where one is more equal than the other for purposes of safety and learning. We hope that one will be the parent.

It is important not to confuse the physical energy and activity of the Orange child with hyperactivity or to give it some other negative label. Orange children live in the body and in sensations. Given firm, respectful care in a safe and challenging environment, active Orange children live joyful, energetic, and productive lives.

Not all Orange children are loud and physically rambunctious. Some are rather quiet and physically still, until they meet a challenge. Then their physical power comes out. And during their quiet times, their Orange humor, competitiveness, and love of freedom are all there, under the surface, awaiting their opportunity to emerge.

Subtleties of emotion, the demands of duty and order, and fine intellectual pursuits are simply not very interesting to Orange children. They live in the same concrete, physical world that Golds prefer. But rather than trying to keep order in this world, Orange children want to have an impact on it. They want to play in it, to be skillful in it, to exercise power over it. Not to talk.

Simple do's and don'ts with natural consequences work best. Orange children will not adapt their behavior based on moral theories or appeals to altruism, but rather on consequences and self-interest. These are things we do and these are things we don't do and here are the consequences either way. Language about right and wrong tends to fall on deaf ears. This can be hard on the Blue and Gold parents whose values tend to be rooted in deeply held beliefs.

Orange children are highly skillful. They learn by doing, by direct physical involvement with things. This is the key to successful education for Orange children. Their senses are keen, and their reactions are quick. They tend to be well muscled and well coordinated. They usually love the outdoors and all physical challenges. Elementary school has been called the "big sit" by Oranges who crave movement. They will accept the "big sit" as long as they can count on recess, lunchtime play, and some hands-on pedagogy. Hard physical effort doesn't faze them as long as it's fun or challenging. Unless they are being forced into some boring physical task, they just want to get better at whatever they do.

Orange children are highly motivated by competition. They love team play and they love to win. They assume that everyone in the game is strong and capable, so they don't lose much sleep over the losers. They hate to lose, but they don't even lose much sleep over their own losses. The Orange child just gets back up and goes at it again.

Orange children love to perform. They enjoy the limelight and want to show others what they can do. They're not much into spectator sports. They want to be on the field, in the thick of things. They know they can do it, and they want the opportunity to prove it.

They have trouble with passive activities like listening and reading. Still, if they have a meaningful goal, they will do whatever it takes to develop the skill and knowledge to achieve it. This is why Orange students really come into their own in the higher grades and in college, where they can follow their interests and choose their goals.

If they are allowed to apply what they learn in action, and if they don't have to wait too long to get that chance, Orange children can endure much. Rote practice and discipline are all right as long as they serve an active purpose. Orange children love change and novelty, but they will put up with repetition if it builds skills and helps get them where they want to go.

In the modern, urban world, Orange children often have a tough time. Our schools, communities, and workplaces are not usually designed for their energetic style. The other Colors have often lost touch with the primordial importance of Orange. Out on the prairies, in the woods, on the sea, in cultures and communities that need tough physical skills, the Orange child is a star on the way to being a really important adult.

THE GREEN CHILD

Green children are born thoughtful. Naturally, not much actual thinking is going for the first few months, but a watchful, inward quality becomes apparent from the beginning. The analytical mind that will emerge has its roots in the quiet, self-contained infant.

Green independence shows itself early. Green children are processing . . . looking, listening, thinking things over, trying to make sense of things. This requires space, time, autonomy. The parent who is expecting immediate intimacy and lots of interaction will be puzzled and sometimes concerned by the Green child.

Green children want to come to a new situation on their own terms with the freedom to move in and out, check things out, compare things with other things, make some tentative judgments, test the judgments, adapt and adjust. They mistrust all quick responses.

The inner workings of the Green child's mind are not easy and fluid. The analytical mind takes things apart, chooses and selects, sees things in chunks, looks for pattern among different elements. This is not the quick approximation and correction of the Orange, the emotional intuitive flow of the Blue, or the orderly application of precedent of the Gold. The Green process takes time, and like any fine instrument, its mechanism is delicate.

This complex inner world is easily thrown off by distractions and confrontations. Green children avoid intrusions. They want to focus. They want to follow their interests where they lead. This is the natural unfolding of their information gathering and analysis. They are capable of being completely absorbed in some investigation for hours, days, even years.

Green children are very inward. Like Blues, they live very much within themselves. Strong emotion is in there, but it can be one of the major intrusions that interfere with the smooth workings of the analytical mind. Green children project a calm and deliberate emotional style most of the time. They tend to be upset by emotions, however, when they arise. Blue children swim in this sea of feelings and keep their heads above water, most of the time. The equally inward Green is subject to being overwhelmed by these feelings. Strong emotions often have a life of their own. They may not be rational, and they can be very difficult to control. Speech chokes up. Tears well up. Confusion sets in. No place to hide. Humiliation. A disaster.

This is further complicated by Green children's need to maintain the integrity of their analysis. This integrity is built into the analytical process. Why should a person analyze if the analysis isn't allowed to determine action? Why think carefully for yourself only to be pushed around by some flood of irrational emotions, whether they are your own or someone else's?

The same basic principle of thinking for themselves leads Green children to question authority and routine at all times. Why? Why? Why? And the explanation had better make some sense. This can be very challenging to a parent who is acting from feeling, from impulse, from tradition, or just trying to get through the day. Green children ask tough questions. Parent and educator might have to learn something in order to answer.

Green children usually seem older than their years. They show that wise, thoughtful demeanor before they can walk. When they start talking, well, it can be a bit unsettling. Not all Green children are geniuses, but they are all thoughtful. They often begin achieving mentally at an early age. They may follow many pathways and interests, and some of them seem strange to the other Colors, like a fascination with bugs or with the inside workings of living things.

Green children don't mind being alone; in fact, they often seek it out. Socializing for its own sake has little interest for them, though they love to talk about whatever does interest them. They are delighted when someone understands and cares—better yet, when someone *knows* something.

They want to be loved and respected like any other child, and like any child, that love needs to be on their own terms. Give them the facts of sexual development as they show curiosity and readiness to find out. Stay with the facts and maybe just a brief statement about what the facts may mean. Long, redundant lectures on any subject are torture to Greens of all ages. Listen for questions both out loud and between the lines. A smothering, emotional approach will close them down and drive them into themselves.

Intellectual challenges are fun for Green children. Rough physical camaraderie may be simply too disorienting, unless the Orange is right there behind the Green. Holidays are okay, but family duties and traditions may feel stultifying.

Both at home and in the classroom, the best approach to Green children includes a lot of watching and listening. Be there, but keep a respectful distance. Challenge them, encourage social contact, but don't interfere too much. Set limits and expect things of them, but don't micromanage. Above all, be willing to learn along with the child in a spirit of calm adventure and safe exploration. Green children need to know that the parent or teacher is there with them and for them, that they belong, that the world is safe so that they can pursue their independent interests.

The next page provides an outline of child needs, strengths, and challenges that should be helpful to parents and teachers, and to anyone who loves children. The following chapter explores the parenting styles of the four Colors.

THE GOLD CHILD

Needs	Strengths	Challenges
Safety	Creating safe space	Risky activities
Security	Organizing	Unpredictability
Stability	Putting things in order	Instability
Organization	Defining appropriate structure	Chaos
Belonging	Fitting into group	Isolation
Participation	Contributing to group/family	Lack of guidance and clear values
Predictability	Serving group order/productivity	Irrational consequences of actions
Continuity	Sustaining group identity and ways	Lack of connection over time
Tradition	Maintaining tradition	Novelty, newness for its own sake
Clear expectations	Meeting expectations	Irrational expectations
Others to be responsible	Setting expectations	Others fail to meet expectations
Rules	Making and supporting rules	Anarchy
Boundaries	Finding and supporting boundaries	Constant change and fluidity
Authority	Supporting/carrying out authority	No one in charge
Roles	Carrying out roles	No defined roles
Responsibilities	Carrying responsibility	No defined responsibility
Work	Working hard	No meaningful work
Appreciation	Thriving on recognition	No sensible recognition
Clear status definition	Supporting clear status definition	Unclear status hierarchy
Permission to relax	Perseverance	Constant pressure to perform

THE BLUE CHILD

Needs	Strengths	Challenges
Encouragement	Giving encouragement/ support	Others' inattention
Support	Able to receive nurture	No structure, arbitrary structure
Nurture	Takes feedback seriously	Others' indifference
Feedback	Gives understanding	Caustic, critical environment
Understanding	Makes self understood	Strong conformity demands
Self-expression	Identifies with group	Balancing expression/ group role
Belonging	Participation	Isolation, alienation
Involvement	Bringing others in	To be seen and not heard
Inclusion	Friendliness	Loss
Friends	Generosity	Aloneness
Honesty	Sensitivity to hidden feelings	Emotionally charged secrets
Harmonious relationships	Imagination	Conflict with others
Others to get along	Peacemaking	Conflict among others
Sensitivity	Intimacy	Stoicism
Pretend play, art, music	Creativity	High expectation of compliance
Flexible structure	Self-management	Routine, impersonal standards
Freedom to be alone	Positive solitude	Enforced participation in conflict
Gentle touch	Loving touch	Rough touch, no touch
Reality checks	Dreaminess	Lack of boundaries, defined roles

THE ORANGE CHILD

Needs	Strengths	Challenges
Independence	Active initiation	Compliance, following
Self-reliance	Autonomy	Blending in
Freedom within limits	Self-motivation	Taking direction
Flexible structure	Thinking on their feet	Accepting structure
Action	Energy	Expectation of quiet/ stillness
Adventure	Risk taking	Being safe
Challenge	Love of the new	Being appropriate
Fun and excitement	Enjoyment	Taking things seriously
Change and variety	Adaptability, flexibility	Managing routine
Attention	Not shy	Attention seeking
Stimulation	Can handle much stimulation at once	Boredom
Hands-on learning	Natural physical understanding	Following the directions
Physical involvement	"Body smart"	Introspection, analysis
Competition	Plenty of drive	Self-sacrifice
Performance	Expressive, daring	Playing anonymous roles
Modeling of skills	Imitation, learning by doing	Taking verbal instruction
Skill practice	Focus (when interested)	Focus (when not interested)
Doing, not watching	Active participation	Quiet observation
Camaraderie	Gregarious	Solitude, working alone
Firm, strong touch	Physicality	Intimate touch
Respectful boundaries	Responds to respect	All arbitrary boundaries

THE GREEN CHILD

Needs	Strengths	Challenges
Rationality	Clear reason	Dealing with the irrational
Time	Perseverance (when interested)	Perseverance (when not interested)
Patience	Takes own sweet time	Hurrying, being hurried
Space	Handles solitude well	Crowding
Autonomy	Thinks for self	Being told
Constant learning opportunities	Love of learning	Rote, repetitive activities
To explore	Loves new experience/ information	Redundancy
Investigation	Loves to inquire	Being fed canned information
Questioning	Needs to see reasons	Accepting things on faith
Explanations	Needs to see cause/ effect	Settling for surface appearances
Challenge	Loves intellectual challenge	Routine
Many interests	Wide-ranging mind	Lack of information resources
Rational authority	Personal integrity	Arbitrary authority
Solitude, social distance	Good at being alone	Enforced social demands
Independence	Self-reliance	Team play
Social encouragement	Learns social skills (if necessary)	Small talk, emotional intimacy
Help with decisions	Complex analysis	Arbitrary deadlines, criteria

CHAPTER 12

Parents

GOLD PARENTS

Commitment and dedication are at the heart of the Gold parenting style. Golds place the highest value on doing important work in life. They often see family and child-rearing as the most important of all work.

For Golds, family values and traditions are the foundation of family life, often of life itself. They expect good order based on proper roles and responsibilities. The traditions are to be respected. Routines and rituals are to be followed with respect. It is this good order that gives safety, predictability, and stability to life.

Great effort and attention are spent in making sure that things are running smoothly and securely. Careful attention is given to details and appearances. Chores are to be done on schedule. Responsibilities are taken seriously. Work and school come first. Privileges are earned, not just taken for granted. Work before play.

As in all areas of life, Gold parents insist on high standards in all things. There are right ways and wrong ways of living and of doing things. Values are central. Life must be held up to the standard. Where it is found wanting, it must be corrected. Constructive criticism is essential.

The Gold parent strives to be a good role model, to lead by example, to be above reproach. This is a tough challenge, and Golds rarely feel that they have measured up. Their answer to this is to redouble their efforts, not to lower the standard. This quality strongly influences their parenting.

For Golds, life is effort. Things that are easy and fun are mistrusted. Feelings and emotions are too unreliable. Clever thinking and analysis can be deceptive. Work is essential. Without work, we have chaos and failure.

Children are expected to carry out their responsibilities and strive for high standards. Parenting must be held to a standard as well. Gold parents must pay attention to all the details. They must make and enforce rules and hold up high expectations. They expect honesty and hard work.

Their parenting style is authoritarian. They are the parents. They are responsible, and they are accountable for the results. It is their job to manage things, to supervise the child for success. A child's failure is the parent's failure, and success comes from doing the right thing.

Organization, planning, routine, punctuality, neatness, a good appearance, respect for tradition, and hard work lead to success. Rewards are appropriate, but they must be earned. Self-worth is a more understandable idea than self-esteem. Self-worth is earned. It doesn't come free.

Discipline is essential, and it is good for the child. It is tied to the values and standards that the Gold parent holds dear. Consequences must be available for misbehavior. Punishment is corrective. It builds character and prepares the child for the rigors of life. Above all, it upholds the standard.

Obedience is required and expected. Gold parents see obedience as belonging to the natural role of the child, just as authority belongs to the role of the parent. Gold parents were usually obedient children. They see this authority of the generations as essential to orderly life. Respect for elders and for those in authority is a key to the stability of the community.

Change must be anticipated and planned for. The child must prepare for each step of the life path. Goals and directions must be established, and action must be directed toward the goals. The parents' duty is to keep the child on track and focused. Children must be involved in appropriate community activities and cultural traditions. Career goals must be set. Social participation and responsibility must be instilled.

Gold parents are often deeply concerned about their dreamy, sensitive Blue children, their impulsive, competitive Orange children, and their independent and skeptical Green children. The right way to live seems so obvious to the Gold. Duty and responsibility, hard work and well-earned rewards make such good sense to them.

Gold parents can be very helpful to their children of other Colors. They can provide a secure base, an orderly foundation upon which the Blue, Orange, or Green children can build their own unique lives.

BLUE PARENTS

For the Blue parent, everything starts with a deep emotional connection with the child. The moment of birth is sacred. Throughout life, contact, communication, and empathy with the child are among the highest values. The responsiveness of the child is very important, and Blue parents take it to heart.

Blues love intensely, and they need to be loved in return. They often hope and expect that their relationship with the child will be the most intimate in their lives. This can lead to pain when the child shows independence, gets angry, rebels, or simply turns away to follow his or her own interests.

We don't get to choose the Colors of our children. The other Colors are not as focused on emotional intimacy as is the Blue parent. Over time, parenting is likely to be an emotional roller coaster for the Blue parent, just like the rest of the Blue life.

Close families based on emotional connection and affection are the Blue ideal. Blues are devoted to family. They invest great energy in the family, often sacrificing their own needs and interests in the process. They expect the same of their spouses and children. To the Blue, family closeness is only natural. Everyone should feel it spontaneously.

Holidays, birthdays, hellos, good-byes, births, deaths, and all the other significant family events are very important to the Blue parent. If someone is really not interested or is going through the motions out of duty, it's deeply troubling to Blue parents. Rejection, coolness, and distance are always troubling for Blues, and these things can really show up around family rituals and important family events.

The family is the most intense arena in life for Blues. Their deep sensitivity makes them particularly vulnerable to the open and hidden conflicts of family life. Marital conflict, trouble between father's family and mother's family, issues with mothers-

and fathers-in-law, sibling rivalry—these are all particularly troubling for Blues.

When things are going well, Blue parents are affectionate, nurturing, emotionally supportive, and enthusiastic. Persons are precious to Blues, and raising children is the cultivation of precious persons. They want to bring out the best in everyone around them. They support the development of true potential in their children, and they value the children's self-expression.

They want to contribute to their child's development, to be important in the child's life and growth. They want to be a positive influence, building self-esteem, nurturing potential, providing emotional safety.

Blue parents rely on the emotional relationship to guide behavior. They try to use as little discipline as possible, preferring to nurture and to guide rather than to structure and provide consequences. They hope and expect that the child will behave well out of love for the parent, high self-esteem, and loyalty to the family.

Conflict is, as always, to be avoided at all costs. Discipline is democratic and personal. Flexibility is valued highly, and whole situations are taken into account. Rigid rules and structures are avoided in favor of serious talks and expressions of concern. This may lead to inconsistency and emotional subjectivity in discipline, and the deep Blue anger and righteous wrath may overflow from time to time.

Sometimes Blue parents use their own pain as a lever to try to influence the child. They may try to act more as a friend and confidant than as an authority figure. Sometimes the child is invited from a very early age to share the emotional trials and tribulations of the Blue parent, and this can be a great burden for the child.

Blues care deeply about their children. They invest great energy and dedication in the work of being a parent. They value differences and support uniqueness, special talents, and special personal qualities. They provide a rich, nurturing environment in which their children can grow and develop.

ORANGE PARENTS

For Orange parents, life is a challenge and an adventure. It is there to be enjoyed. Family life is not about meticulous details, musty traditions, sentimentality, or intellectual discourse. It is about challenge, camaraderie, and fun.

Children should be raised to be strong, independent, self-reliant, and resilient. They don't need to be fawned over, organized, or analyzed. They need to play, to do their own thing. Children don't need constant attention from their parents, and Orange parents must have their own freedom if they are to be healthy and happy.

The Orange home is a relaxed and casual environment. It may be very spare, almost unimportant—a place to eat and sleep, a base of operations for action and adventure in the wider world. It may be a work of art with all kinds of unique and original furnishings and architecture. Or it may be a complex playground full of workshops, awash in the clutter of hobbies and games, a gymnasium, or grand central station for the entire neighborhood.

Orange parents communicate this sense of openness and action to their children. They must live this way themselves, and they wish to carry their children right along with them. They are optimistic, flexible, and here-and-now-oriented. They love to laugh, and they avoid dark, heavy intellectual or emotional experiences.

Boredom is the enemy. Routine and ritual have no appeal. Family gatherings are not about duty and sentiment. They are about fun. Change and action are the order of the day. Oranges love change, novelty, variety. Each day is a new opportunity to try new things.

The Orange emotional life is about involvement and camaraderie. Oranges are usually quite social, and the Orange family is usually a hub of activity. Big families are common, with lots of visiting back and forth. Parenting is a shared project. Everyone is involved. Aunts and uncles, grandparents, family friends, all are invited to care for the children.

Competition is part of everything. Orange parents love to challenge their children, to play hard and build strength and power. Winning is important in play and in life, but in a funny way it's less important to Oranges than to the other Colors. It doesn't have the personal quality that it has for Blues. It doesn't mean order versus chaos as it may for Golds. It doesn't suggest disorienting failure the way it may for Greens.

Work is done in spurts of tremendous energy. It is not approached as an ongoing daily routine, to be kept up with moment by moment. Get a Dumpster and clean the house in a day. Make it a game. Get everyone in the neighborhood involved. Invite the family. Door prizes!

As stated before, Oranges love skill, and they will work hard in a focused way to develop it. But it must be useful skill. Orange parents love to teach skills, and they show by doing all the time with their children. Skill in action is the highest value for the Orange. They want their children to be as good as they can be at whatever interests them.

Orange parents aren't committed to any particular way of parenting, preferring to deal with things as they come along. They are not consistent disciplinarians, but they do expect to be obeyed. They tend to rely on their personal power and direct, immediate solutions, rather than on routines, emotional connectedness, or reasoning. They would rather not have to discipline at all, and rarely plan how they will do it.

When the need to discipline pops up in a situation, Orange parents respond in terms of the immediate circumstances. They are not troubled by routine misbehavior. They like pluckiness and mischief, and they respect children's willfulness as strength. It is only when the children are really at serious risk, or when they are disrupting the parent's life, that discipline becomes an issue.

Oranges are often quick to anger, and just as quick to forgive and forget. They tend to be somewhat manipulative themselves, and they see through children's manipulations fairly easily. It's hard to con an Orange. They try to keep things light and humorous, laughing off troubles as much as possible, and they separate easily when their children are ready to be on their own.

Orange parents give their children an energetic and creative home environment full of fun and action. The Blue child may find it somewhat emotionally stressful. The Gold child may try to parent the Orange parent and stabilize things in the family. The Green child may pull back and watch. But all the children will get the message. Life is short. Do something!

GREEN PARENTS

Green parents are thoughtful, parenting with reason and rationality. They often read books and apply parenting methods that make sense to them. They want to know what the experts have to say, but they will think the problem through for themselves before deciding how to act.

Green parents are very interested in the growth and development of the child, particularly his or her intellectual and educational development. Life is about learning and understanding. It is about curiosity, interests, exploration, experiment, and information.

Motivation comes from within for Greens. They expect their children to have interests that will guide their lives. They talk things over and draw out the children's interests, feeding them and nurturing them with opportunities to learn.

They love to question and to challenge the child's understanding, opening up new pathways and new ideas. Intellectual discussion is play, and they love to see children move toward their full creative potential. They love intellectual games, puns and plays on words, complex puzzles, and *Jeopardy!*

Green parents give a high value to competency, to rigorous understanding and careful application of principles. They expect their children to think about consequences before they act—to use their heads. Thoughtlessness and stupidity are the great sins. "God put a wonderful brain in your head. It isn't there just to hold up your hair and keep your ears apart. Your highest duty is to use it."

Greens are skeptical and independent by nature. They do not accept authority easily themselves, and they do not impose it easily on their children either. Greens prefer reason and logic to rules and consequences. They give reasons for their decisions. They prefer to give information that will guide their children's decisions, to influence rather than enforce.

Green parents try to be logical, objective, and fair. They listen to the facts of the case. Weigh the possible outcomes and consequences. They are not in a hurry. They want to talk things over and be sure before going ahead. They are not moved by impulses, emotionalism, or tradition. They want the facts, and they question the facts, too.

Greens refuse to quarrel. Discussion is a high art. It is to be carried out in a reasonable and respectful way. They have no patience, however, for obvious stupidity. They don't "suffer fools gladly," as the old saying goes. They can be quite acid-tongued and sarcastic about foolishness. When someone has acted stupidly and the consequences are happening, well, that's just how it works, doesn't it? Learn from it.

As parents, Greens can be prone to lecturing. The Blue, Gold, or Orange child may become somewhat deaf to the Green logic. Green parents are often at a loss about what to do with a highly emotional Blue child, a stubborn Gold child, or a willful Orange one. When reason fails, the Green parent may simply withdraw. Strong, authoritarian interventions may be just too unsettling.

Autonomy is a very high value to Greens. People shouldn't have to be pushed, ordered about, or bossed. Intellectual freedom, freedom of speech, choice, and thought are essential. The Green parent may feel that it is best for children to just learn from consequences rather than to be forced against their will.

Green parents rely on clear communication of important information. Confusion is seen as the main source of trouble. If the facts are clear, action can be clear. Learning can take place. A rational critique of someone's thinking or behavior is an expression of caring. Repetition should not be necessary. Once a thing has been pointed out, then that should be enough.

As stated before, emotions run deep for Greens, but they are very uneasy about communicating them. They deeply mistrust what they see as easy emotionalism. Constant expressions of love, appreciation, pride, and praise in a family seem false and intrusive to Greens. They expect people to infer their caring and appreciation from their investment and commitment. This emotional stoicism drives Blues nuts.

Green parents expose their children to the deep questions about life. They bring to their families the life of the mind. They are democratic, rational, and open-minded, and they bring out the natural curiosity and creativity of their children.

PARENT STRENGTHS AND CHALLENGES

Gold Parent Strengths	Gold Parent Challenges
Responsible	Being flexible
Dedicated	Accepting differences
Stable	Sharing authority
Family-oriented	Dealing with uncertainty
Hardworking	Responding to change
Helpful	Dealing with rebellion
Good role model	Dealing with irresponsibility
Authoritative	Supporting creativity
Strong values	Handling emotional sensitivity
Clear expectations	Dealing with noise and confusion
Values rules	Handling lack of appreciation
Establishes routines	Handling disrespect
Traditional	Playing and being spontaneous
Organized	
Practical	
Objective	

Blue Parent Strengths	Blue Parent Challenges
Nurturing	Exercising authority
Devoted	Setting limits and boundaries
Emotionally sensitive	Dealing with conflict
Values closeness	Dealing with loss
Values persons	Saying good-bye
Good communication	Handling rejection
Supports potential	Being disliked or criticized
Encourages self-expression	Being consistent
Harmonious in relationships	Being objective
Builds family cohesion	Putting needs before wants
Flexible	Putting business before feelings
Democratic	
Disciplines through caring	
Warm	
Enthusiastic	
Spiritual	
Noncompetitive	

Orange Parent Strengths	Orange Parent Challenges
Optimistic	Being consistent
Flexible	Exercising authority
Direct	Planning and organizing
Accepting	Handling time and schedules
Loves change	Attending to duties
Adventurous	Putting work before play
Relaxed	Encouraging neatness
Casual	Being emotionally sensitive
Nonjudgmental	Being serious
Friendly	Being intellectual
Engaged	Being patient

Emotionally strong	Handling quick anger
Here and now	
Hands on	
Playful *and* hardworking	
Expects obedience	

Green Parent Strengths	Green Parent Challenges
Logical	Exercising authority
Objective	Enforcing limits and boundaries
Emotionally calm	Making firm decisions
Uses guidance and influence	Avoiding too much lecturing
Uses information	Avoiding sarcasm and withdrawal
Uses parenting methods	Dealing with illogic
Gives reasons	Dealing with rebellion
Thinks things through	Communicating feelings
Pays attention to cause/effect	Handling others' emotions
Uses independent judgment	Noise and distraction
Values growth	Confusion and conflict
Encourages development	Handling details, time pressure
Proud of accomplishments	Social participation
Intellectually stimulating	
Sets high intellectual standards	
Uses natural consequences	

TEACHING AND LEARNING STYLES

Gold Teaching Style	Gold Student Learning Needs
Strong work ethic	Order and structure
Clear routine	Clear expectations and directions
Lots of structure	Goals and action sequences
Repetition and practice	Specific content

Well-organized activities
Traditional learning content
Emphasis on community traditions
Emphasis on appearances and propriety
Detailed, tried-and-true lesson plans
Demand for student accountability
Use of text, precedents, references
Strict and firm discipline

Repetition and practice
Learning from the foundation up
Freedom from mess and confusion
Responsibility and authority
Visible recognition and rewards
Consistent discipline
Justice based on rules and authority

Blue Teaching Style

High participation
Personal encouragement
Emotional safety
Affection
Physical contact
Emphasis on the positive
Individualized learning
Variety
Creativity
Inspiration and aspiration
Cooperation over competition
Expects motivation through self-actualization
Discipline through understanding
Emphasis on fairness

Blue Student Learning Needs

Emotional safety
Harmonious relationships
Personal encouragement and recognition
Openness and interaction
Group learning in a safe atmosphere
Minimum conflict
Inspiration, exploration, creativity
Personal expression
External challenge/structure
Conceptual/global learning
Personal fairness
Discipline based on understanding/inclusion

Orange Teaching Style

Spontaneous
Free-flowing structure
Relevant

Orange Student Learning Needs

Competition
Immediacy
Application of learning

Here and now
Applied
Concrete
Immediate
Hands-on
Action
Variety
Novelty
Challenge
Upbeat competition
Humor and fun
Situational discipline
Control through personal power

Skills over knowledge
Action over talking/listening
Movement over sitting
Learning by doing
Discovery
Variety of experience
Camaraderie
Firm, respectful, consistent discipline
External structure

Green Teaching Style

Lecture/dialogue
Explanation
Theory
Critical analysis
Exploration
Independent thinking
Skepticism
Expects motivation based on interest
Values student autonomy
Emphasizes personal responsibility
Disciplines through guidance/suggestion
Uses natural consequences
Reluctant to enforce structure

Green Student Learning Needs

Understanding of cause and effect; "Why, why, why?"
Exposure to concepts/ideas
Time for thought
Freedom to doubt/question
Teacher patience
Time to answer questions
Independent learning challenges
Relevance
Recognition of capabilities
Minimum repetition/redundancy
Reality checks and timelines
Minimum forced intimacy or participation
Rational discipline
Natural consequences

CHAPTER 13

Moving Forward with the Colors

Understanding the natural differences between and among people will be useful to you in different ways depending upon your Color mixture. As we have seen throughout the book, the motivations and rewards that are meaningful to each Color differ in predictable ways.

Those of us with considerable Blue in our temperament will tend to see the wholeness and balance of the differences as beautiful and deeply meaningful. We will resist any tendency to pigeonhole our fellow creatures. At the same time, we will rejoice in the detailed exploration and rich appreciation of human differences that Colors makes possible. For Blues, it is a joy to discover these new ways to find and highlight the value of persons, and to contribute to the blossoming in health and delight of "children and other living things," as the saying goes. We will also find new ways to appreciate the other Colors whose priorities and ways of life may have seemed so mysterious and even harsh to the Blue heart. In addition, Colors gives us permission and puts a much-needed blessing upon our sensitivity and emotionality. Especially for the Blue men among us, it is of great value to let go of the stiff upper lip and swim freely in the sea of emotion.

For those of us who are deeply rooted in Gold, the value of the

Colors will have a more practical aspect. Golds will probably still be irritated by Blue sentimentality, Green studiousness and vacillation, and Orange rambunctiousness. Still, by virtue of understanding the inevitability of these qualities, Golds will be able to focus on finding keys to cooperation that work for the good of the tradition, the family, the community, or the project.

One metaphor that Golds often find helpful is to see the temperaments of other people as being akin to the weather. Indeed, this weather metaphor can be helpful to all the Colors. We can all waste enormous time and energy complaining about the weather, but how much more efficient it is simply to dress appropriately for whatever weather comes our way. Very important for us as Golds, then, is the growing understanding of ourselves that Colors brings, the permission it offers for us to be who we are with our emphasis on serious matters, our focus on good order, work, and traditional values, and the high standards that we impose upon ourselves and others.

When we are deeply Green by nature, we are usually very skeptical of any attempt to categorize us. Of all the Colors, we tend to be the most aware of our own uniqueness, and it has great value to us. We look forward at the end of our days to looking back over a life lived in our own authentic way. At first, Colors may seem to threaten that authenticity. In the end, however, we see that Colors blesses our differences and our Green authenticity. In addition, as Colors reveals itself to us as Greens, we begin to realize its power as a tool in analyzing others. Through this pathway, we often find its value in helping us understand and accept ourselves.

Colors can be a bridge for us as Greens in finding our way into the inner life of others. Most of us have rarely sought deep intimacy, though we may be interested in understanding others. Our inner world is precious to us, and it is not to be cheapened by a lot of glib chitchat and emotional sharing. Still, we do need to know and understand others in order to pursue our ends and make our contribution to the community, and it is here that Colors can help by shedding light upon the inner world of others. In addition, Colors helps others understand and accept us as we are. It lets the other Colors know how deeply we do feel and how much we do care, but without the embarrassing and unpleasant process of self-disclosure.

For those of us who are filled with that wonderful energy called Orange, Colors gives us the permission that we have needed all our lives. "Sit down, hush up, slow down, grow up, don't be so immature, think before you act!" Unless we are very lucky Oranges, we have felt entirely too much of this thumb of oppression pushing down on us. Okay, so we need to take some of this advice, fine! Every Color needs to have its extremes checked and corrected to some degree, doesn't it? That's at least partly what relationships are all about—finding good balance.

In these and in many other ways, Colors has its special payoffs for each of us. Its special blend of payoffs will be finely tuned to our own balance of personal qualities. It's amazing how much you will be able to tell about the people you meet as you listen and watch their Colors unfold. Their politics, their pleasures and preferences, their ways of relating—all become rather transparent.

This is, of course, part of the fun and the positive value of Colors, but it also raises a challenge. My suggestion to everyone I talk to about this is to go easy, to be gentle, and above all, to work on letting go of your prejudices against your lowest Colors. I think this is the best advice of all. If you can love your lowest Color when you find it in yourself and others, I assure you, you will gain the maximum value from your understanding of Colors . . . and you will do the least harm.

LESSONS LEARNED: NEWFOUND RESPECT

The Colors will always be with and around you. If Golds drive you nuts, try learning to have sympathy and concern for their heavy burdens. Try to understand the ways they don't live up to their own expectations. Notice the pain that this brings them, even when they're expecting others to do what they themselves can't. Learn to value their contribution to all the efforts they are engaged in. Then you will be able to get along in a friendly and effective way with Golds. You will be able to see what their deep concerns and responsibilities are and lend a hand. This will endear you to Golds more than any other thing. Help them with whatever really concerns them. That's the key to getting along with Gold.

If the Blues make you crazy with their emotionalism and endless talk about relationships, try to appreciate the sensitivity they bring to the process of the community, the way they soften the edges and humanize the expectations. Help them feel emotionally safe and valuable as people. Then they will give heart and soul to whatever projects or activities you may be engaged in. Appreciate their vulnerability. Above all, however, show a little vulnerability yourself. This is the real key with Blues. Allow some of your own softness and uncertainty to show through, and you'll bring out trust and support from them. As they often say to me: "When you show your vulnerability, it brings out the best in me."

On the other hand, if all they see is your armor, they will resist you and defend themselves, expecting pain.

If Oranges are just too rambunctious and playful for your taste, try sitting back and observing their energy for a while. Notice where it is focused. Learn to appreciate how they direct and channel all that voltage. Learn from them to find some of that power in yourself. This last part can be a tough challenge for each of the other Colors, but Oranges really respond to the Orange in others. Good strong physical presentation, high-fives, team energy, and—above all—mutual respect will win Oranges' acceptance and affection. It will bring out their respect for you and motivate them to give their very best participation. It is one of the key messages of the whole Colors experience that Orange is not immaturity waiting to grow up! Orange is a valid adult style, a natural quality that is predominant in as much as a third of the population as a whole. Oranges don't need another lecture on character development. They need to be respected, and they need strong, direct, respectful communication.

If Green is your lowest Color, and if the cool, detached, intellectual style of Greens is hard for you to take, the key to dealing with it is to learn to learn. Learn to love to learn! Even if it's just during those times when you are with Green folks, become a fellow student with them. Learn from them. Learn with them. Share something you have learned (but be sure to let them share what they know about the subject as well). This is the ground upon which they can meet you. In learning, they feel a degree of social safety. This is the ground upon which they will feel most able to open up. Once you get some rapport established through shared learning, then you may be able to shift the ground a bit to your feelings, your responsibilities, or your playfulness. Until Greens feel sure that their intelligence and information will be respected, they won't feel safe with the strengths of the other Colors. When you think about it, this is the key for all of us. Until we know that our own strength is valued, we won't want to show our weakness.

Ultimately, with an understanding of Colors come new responsibilities. We know people's strengths by knowing their temperament, but we may also learn something of their weaknesses and vulnerabilities. How we use this understanding is an ethical challenge to which each of us must respond.

As a final note, I like to remember that the Yup'ik Eskimo symbol places the four different Color elements around the edge of the hoop—but the middle of the hoop, the very center of things, is left open for the spirit, for the soul, for the clarity of life itself, in which there is no Color. In this way of thinking, spirit is neither heart nor body nor intellect nor duty. Spirit is what underlies and enfolds them all, and watched from the perspective of that center, our understanding of the lesser qualities of our personalities can shed much light on our lives and behavior.

It seems to me that the four Colors, seasoned and illuminated by the spirit, provide a rich, broad, and meaningful map of human life. And in the end, it seems that *Living Our Colors* means really, fully living our lives.

Appendix: Extra Quiz Sheets

A Colors Quiz:

Rank the four sets of words in each item **4, 3, 2, or 1** according to how well they describe you. **(4 is most like you.)**

1. a. _____ solid, steady, careful
b. _____ feeling, sympathetic, kind
c. _____ cool, clever, independent
d. _____ lively, witty, energetic

2. a. _____ reasonable, moral, hard-working
b. _____ sensitive, sincere, caring
c. _____ logical, abstract, moral
d. _____ skillful, playful, fun-loving

3. a. _____ dependable, faithful, devoted
b. _____ close, personal, involved
c. _____ curious, scientific, thoughtful
d. _____ daring, energetic, brave

4. a. _____ reliable, organized, serious
b. _____ peaceful, harmonious, warm
c. _____ impatient, perfectionist, heady
d. _____ here-and-now, impulsive, active

5. a. _____ consistent, structured, planned
b. _____ meaningful, spiritual, inspired
c. _____ analyzing, testing, model-making
d. _____ high-impact, persuasive, generous

6. a. _____ sane, faithful, supportive
b. _____ poetic, musical, artistic
c. _____ theoretical, studious, principled
d. _____ performing, playing, creating

7. a. _____ commit, follow-through, persist
b. _____ communicate, encourage, nurture
c. _____ inform, discuss, question
d. _____ energize, compete, engage

8. a. _____ conserve, maintain, protect
b. _____ inspire, understand, appreciate
c. _____ design, invent, construct
d. _____ promote, excite, activate

9. a. _____ value, honor, provide
b. _____ share, connect, express
c. _____ respect, stimulate, dialogue
d. _____ touch, pleasure, surprise

10. a. _____ traditional, loyal, conservative
b. _____ belonging, involved, cooperative
c. _____ skeptical, non-conforming, fair
d. _____ free, independent, rebellious

Totals

a. Gold _____ **b. Blue** _____ **c. Green** _____ **d. Orange** _____

A Colors Quiz:

Rank the four sets of words in each item **4, 3, 2, or 1** according to how well they describe you. **(4 is most like you.)**

1. a. _____ solid, steady, careful
   b. _____ feeling, sympathetic, kind
   c. _____ cool, clever, independent
   d. _____ lively, witty, energetic

2. a. _____ reasonable, moral, hard-working
   b. _____ sensitive, sincere, caring
   c. _____ logical, abstract, moral
   d. _____ skillful, playful, fun-loving

3. a. _____ dependable, faithful, devoted
   b. _____ close, personal, involved
   c. _____ curious, scientific, thoughtful
   d. _____ daring, energetic, brave

4. a. _____ reliable, organized, serious
   b. _____ peaceful, harmonious, warm
   c. _____ impatient, perfectionist, heady
   d. _____ here-and-now, impulsive, active

5. a. _____ consistent, structured, planned
   b. _____ meaningful, spiritual, inspired
   c. _____ analyzing, testing, model-making
   d. _____ high-impact, persuasive, generous

6. a. _____ sane, faithful, supportive
   b. _____ poetic, musical, artistic
   c. _____ theoretical, studious, principled
   d. _____ performing, playing, creating

7. a. _____ commit, follow-through, persist
   b. _____ communicate, encourage, nurture
   c. _____ inform, discuss, question
   d. _____ energize, compete, engage

8. a. _____ conserve, maintain, protect
   b. _____ inspire, understand, appreciate
   c. _____ design, invent, construct
   d. _____ promote, excite, activate

9. a. _____ value, honor, provide
   b. _____ share, connect, express
   c. _____ respect, stimulate, dialogue
   d. _____ touch, pleasure, surprise

10. a. _____ traditional, loyal, conservative
    b. _____ belonging, involved, cooperative
    c. _____ skeptical, non-conforming, fair
    d. _____ free, independent, rebellious

Totals

a. Gold _____ **b. Blue** _____ **c. Green** _____ **d. Orange** _____

Memo Jasso Brown's Studio

TOM MADDRON, a graduate from the University of Oregon with a Master of Science in Counseling Psychology, has made his living first as a marriage, child, and family therapist, and then traveling and training human relations skills in business, education, and social services. Known as the "Colors Guy," he has explored the personality styles of thousands of persons of all walks of life. He lives with his wife, Peggy, a teacher, in the coastal town of North Bend, Oregon.